Heaven to Earth

Anthony Mangun

ISBN-10: 1727645413
ISBN-13:   978-1727645415

DEDICATION

TO MY WIFE, MICKEY

Life would not be life without you! Your love and care for me is deeper and wider than I can even fathom. The decades of "us" go down in history as the best years of my life. *You will always be my inspiration.*

TO MY PARENTS

To my Dad, G. A. Mangun, for sharing this story with me first. For the example and legacy you left for me, I will forever be grateful. I miss you every day.

To my Mother, Vesta Layne Mangun – The wealth of knowledge and timeless love you give me every day is matchless. The example you set in daily prayer, in personal evangelism, in loving God and loving people guides my life.

TO MY CHILDREN and GRANDCHILDREN

Miquell and Jeff – Kind, compassionate, fervent, selfless, full of life and love…*you fill my heart.* The unbreakable bond we share grows stronger every day. Though states and miles separate us, we remain woven together. And so we shall.

Gentry and Lexie – *You have given me such joy.* The blending and merging of your lives has been nothing less than miraculous. The fact you've been elected to succeed me in serving and shepherding the greatest people in the world speaks well of you and makes me eternally grateful.

Eva and Gibson – *When I think of you, I smile.* My prayer for you both is that you will treasure your heritage and walk boldly into a limitless future, building His kingdom and living the principles of prayer and the Word that have been exampled before you.

ACKNOWLEDGMENTS

TO MY BELOVED POA

The Pentecostals of Alexandria – the church family I love and have served for almost four decades. Some of you were privileged to learn this prayer plan from our Bishop before you heard it from me. You have practiced it in your prayer rooms, both at the church and in private places. You live out the evidence of its success.

TO MY DEAR FRIEND

For friendship that spans decades, for years and the most brilliant of minds willingly shared. Thank you, Mike Williams, for everything always.

TO MY ASSISTANT

Thanks to Pamela Nolde, for taking all the pieces and putting them together…for the research and skill that took spoken words, typed notes, and preaching DVDs that helped create this book. Mickey and I would not look or sound nearly as good without you in our lives. Please live forever.

TO OTHERS

Thanks to Teryn Spears and numerous gifted individuals who left their hand, and heart print, on *Heaven to Earth* – investing their expertise in everything from editing to artwork in this labor of love and celebration of prayer. You know who you are, and so do I.

CONTENTS

FOREWORD

When during a chance conversation in North Carolina, a mutual friend suggested I attend a camp meeting the following week, in Tioga, Louisiana, no less, it was because – in his words – I needed to know Anthony Mangun, and he needed to know me. It seemed incidental, certainly not material to my future in ministry, which we were discussing. These forty-eight years later, it is obvious that it was anything but – incidental, that is.

With regard to friendship, C.S. Lewis said, *We think we have chosen our peers. But, for a Christian, there are, strictly speaking, no chances.* He allowed as to how the same Christ Who had told His disciples, *Ye have not chosen Me, but I have chosen you,* can as well say to us – *Ye have not chosen one another, but I have chosen you for one another.*[1] It is not chance, but choice – Divine choice – that links our lives. And after a near half-century of doing ministry together, Anthony Mangun remains as passionate and prolific an advocate for the practice of prayer as I have ever had the privilege to hear.

In that pursuit, on the pages that follow, Pastor Mangun allows us to eavesdrop on a series of conversations with his father, during which the senior, G.A. Mangun – a powerful, prophetic preacher of the gospel in his own right – reveals the **Tabernacle of Moses** to be a template for communication, between Maker and man.

To be sure, we are all haunted by the call, indeed command, to pray – to pray fervently, and without ceasing. But just as surely, many – if not most of us – wonder *when* to pray, *where* to pray, *what* to pray, *how long* to pray.

Notwithstanding the Father's promise to hear, and heed our pleas, we struggle with how to make those conversations with our Creator meaningful to ourselves, and the Almighty as well. Thus for some, even faithful believers, there exists a great gulf between deed and desire.

People who pray, stand on promises that are little more than puzzling pronouncements, to those who do not. Face to face with the futility of life – on earth, in time – these raise the white flag. Not because He is not able, but for failing to ask!

In *Heaven To Earth,* the author provides us a path out of the suffocating superficiality of a life without prayer. The apostle Paul lamented as to how, *To will is present,* but *to do* is something else altogether.[2] On these pages, Pastor Mangun suggests a paradigm of prayer, that is sure to set even the most prayerless disciple free from that kind of ual duplicity.

When prayer is the subject, our good intentions, noble aims, and earnest desires, all add up to nothing – they make no difference at all – unless, and until something, or someone provokes us to pray. The obvious biblical pattern for prayer that follows, takes the mystery out of this most basic of Christian disciplines, while building a compelling case for communion with God.

Contemplating God's greatness, the Messianic prophet Isaiah challenged us to, *Lift up your eyes on high, and behold Who hath created these things.*[3] Despite the beauty and brilliance of billions of flaming stars filling the constellations above us, when the Creator was ready to take credit for creating them – the stars – He only used five (5) words: *He made the stars also.*[4]

But that same God – *Author and Finisher of our faith*[5] – devoted no fewer than fifty (50) chapters of the Bible's sixty-six inspired books to a description, and discussion, of the **Tabernacle of Moses.**[6]

So we do well, to learn these blessed truths, and in so doing bring ... *Heaven To Earth.*

Michael Jesse Williams

---

1. The Four Loves, C.S. Lewis
2. Romans 7:18
3. Isaiah 40:26
4. Genesis 1:16
5. Hebrews 12:2
6. Biblecharts.org

PROLOGUE

It seems the only way to start telling the story of Heaven to Earth is for me to share with you some history of the man who shared it with me. He was my father. He was a great man of God with keen insight into the Word. He also had an ability to take the Word and "bring it home" – making it fit in practical applications into the lives of the people he led. So it was with tabernacle prayer. His story, briefly told here, will give you a glimpse of why and how he became the man of God he was. His name was G. A. Mangun.

Dad was born on March 11, 1919 in LaPaz, Indiana. He was the second of six and the only son born to Walter and Bertha Mangun. Months after my father's birth, my grandparents had miraculous personal conversion experiences and themselves became pioneers of the New Birth message. Their ministry would shape the lives of their children, while changing the lives of those to whom they ministered.

In telling his life story, my father often shared about an experience that occurred when he was only eight years old. His younger sister, Ruth, was diagnosed with diphtheria. Word had reached my grandparents that Sister Manny Crawford was holding a healing campaign in South Bend, Indiana. The family made the journey to that town and found themselves in a place with walls covered by left-behind wheelchairs, crutches, and canes. It was obviously a place of physical healing.

Before they could get the sick baby girl out of the car, though, the evangelist stepped out and told my grandfather, "Take her home. She's healed." My dad admitted he was a little disbelieving, at least at first. He recalled saying or at least thinking, "Healed, my foot! She's dead!" He was wrong. Ruth was healed! God was building a foundation of prayer, of faith, and of miraculous signs and wonders, of the Spirit, in my father's life. For the decades to come, Dad would often refer to that incident as one that changed his life forever.

Another pivotal point in my father's life story occurred in 1939 when he was working a sales route in northern and central Indiana. He returned to his home in Kokomo, Indiana and received word that his mother was dying. He immediately made the needed travel arrangements to go to her. It was while traveling that my Dad made a promise to God – a bargain some would call it. If God would heal his mother, he would surrender his life to God and do whatever God wanted him to do. He happened to look at his watch at the end of his prayer. It was straight up midnight.

When he reached home a few hours later, his mother was fine. She had been instantly healed during the night hours. It was a few weeks later my grandmother told my father about that fateful night when death seemed so near. Yet, at precisely midnight the Lord touched and healed her instantly.

Our church printed a wonderful memorial booklet for my father's home-going service. It included the following personal account of what came next. Several weeks had passed since my grandmother's miraculous healing. Dad was attending a revival in Kokomo, Indiana and had his own midnight hour experience. In his own words:

> I don't know what the preacher was preaching. But when he got done, I went down into the basement and knelt at a cane-bottom chair at twenty minutes

14

before ten o'clock. I lifted up my hands for two hours and twenty minutes. I never let those hands come down – I held them up. I looked up at Jesus dying on the cross. I could have held my hands up the rest of the night. I fell on my back, and when I did, I began to speak in a beautiful language for about twenty minutes. I tried to come back into English and couldn't. I said, "This beats anything I've ever seen." I couldn't come back into English because I was speaking in tongues.

There was a roomful of people when I started, but there were two people when I finished. When I walked out of that basement, I looked up. The moon was shining, stars were twinkling. The trees were waving and shouting glory. The glory of the Lord shone in my life there probably the most abundant of any time I have ever experienced.

The scripture tells us "The steps of a good man are ordered by the Lord..." (Psalm 37:23). My father's ordered-by-God steps took him to St. Paul, Minnesota, where he learned and practiced the disciplines of prayer and fasting. During this time he averaged four days a week in fasting. He spent extended hours each day in prayer.

From Bible College to the preaching circuit, my father evangelized, preaching the Gospel from Minnesota to Louisiana to Ohio and back to Louisiana. His first real breakthrough came in a little town called Eros, Louisiana. It was there that many miracles occurred, and approximately 60 people received the Holy Ghost.

It was the next step in my Dad's evangelistic journey that was going to be a giant step in the journey of his life. After Eros, his next stop was Diboll, Texas. My maternal grandfather, Reverend

R. D. Gibson, was pastoring nearby. In those days, if one church in the area had an evangelist many of the other churches would join them for services. So it was in this series of meetings, my father would meet my mother, a beautiful 17-year-old girl named Vesta Layne Gibson. The meeting was the stuff of destiny, and the subsequent days, weeks, and months were the kind of courtship only God could orchestrate.

My dad was fascinated by the young lady who came into the building and "worked the room" touching and smiling and connecting with everyone, especially the elders. It might well have been "love at first sight." When it came time for my father to move on to his next revival, he asked mother if perhaps they could write letters to one another. She agreed.

Mother remembers this about their exchange of letters: "There was no romance; it was just how many had received the Holy Ghost, how many had been baptized in Jesus name, how the revival was going, and to be sure and pray. Then those letters began to express a 'special request' he wanted us to pray about."

Eventually, my father proposed marriage, my mother accepted, and they were married. From that point forward they were about the work of the kingdom and ever giving themselves to prayer and fasting. It was not just something they taught, it was something they lived.

My parents were passionate about evangelism and highly successful in that area of ministry. There were more invitations than time. There were countless stories of deliverance, healing, salvation, changed hearts, and changed lives. They were doing what they had been called to do.

When the call came to possibly become a pastor, the response was not an immediate or resounding "yes!" Instead, dad specifically prayed, "Lord, I don't want to pastor…" When he talked with mother about the possibility of leaving the work of the evangelist and taking on the role of pastor, her response was equal to his: "No, thank you, please!" However, my parents also knew their commitment to God was stronger than their personal preferences. If God said, "Go" they would indeed go wherever they were called and do whatever God asked them to do.

The possibility of becoming pastor seemed to be constantly in front of them. The urging of the Spirit could not be ignored. What my parents wanted was clear; what God was calling them to do was clearer. Ultimately, what He wanted was what they wanted and their answer became "Yes!" to His will and to His way. It was a "yes!" to becoming a pastor – and a "yes!" to Alexandria, Louisiana.

Elected by 38 voting members, our family – now comprised of my father, mother, and me at 6 months of age – relocated to Alexandria, Louisiana. My parents promptly set about making their little band of believers into a mighty army of prayer warriors. They prayed. They fasted. They preached the Word. The foundational truths of the Kingdom that directed the days of their lives were clear: Pray one hour a day. Fast one day a week. Win souls.

The church in Alexandria grew. My parents' ministry grew. The years passed and the principles of prayer and fasting continued to be part-and-parcel of their message to anyone and everyone who sought a relationship with Jesus Christ. Whether you were a new convert or a seasoned saint, the power of prayer and fasting was not just taught to you at The Greater First United Pentecostal Church (what would later become The Pentecostals of Alexandria), it was lived before you every day.

After evangelizing, and pastoring in Plano, Texas, in May of 1981 I returned to Alexandria with my own family of three in tow – me, my wife, Mickey, and our daughter, Miquell – to become pastor and serve alongside my parents. The things that had been integral to their ministry remained integral to mine. Prayer. Fasting. Winning souls. These things did not – have not – and will not – diminish. What was integral to the life of my father is still lived out in the lives of the myriad people who felt the influence of his ministry, as well as in my own life and ministry.

We don't know exactly when or how it happened, we just know it did. Through prayer and study of the Word, and more prayer and fasting, and more study still my father developed, in his own prayer life, a plan of prayer that followed the outline of the Tabernacle of Moses. Others had done it before him. He took previous patterns and added his own unique flair.

In the later years of my father's life and ministry praying through the tabernacle became more and more central to his daily prayer life. Sometimes Dad would spend an entire day, slowly and methodically making his way from the Entrance Gate of praise and thanksgiving to the Holy of Holies where he could bask in the shekinah glory and presence of Almighty God. Some days it went much faster than that, and he could pray completely through the plan in an hour or less. Yet, always he was praying and most often he was somewhere in this plan.

Dad shared the lesson of tabernacle prayer with me. He shared the lesson with his church. The unique day came when he was even able to share the lesson with his only grandson, my son, Gentry. Now, I am honored to put it in writing and share it with you.

We know the concept of a tabernacle prayer plan is not unique to my father or his prayer life. His influence and his prayers had an impact on his family and his church that can only be measured in eternity. This book is not intended to be a scholarly dissertation on the Tabernacle Plan, nor even a comprehensive study of prayer. It is simply the story of my father's lifestyle of prayer. We now, through this book, take his lifestyle and legacy a step further and invite you to join us – as we were privileged to join him – in praying the tabernacle.

Anthony Mangun

CHAPTER ONE

chapter one

THE TABERNACLE STORY

God is a God of detail.

Science tells us there are over one hundred million stars in our galaxy alone – and that there may be over one hundred and twenty-five more galaxies in the universe with equal or more stars in each (http://imagine.gsfc. nasa. gov). Psalms 147:4 (*King James Version*) tells us He not only numbers the stars, but "…he calleth them all by their names." That's detail.

Take a walk through a garden or a forest, and try to count the different shades of green. That's detail.

Genesis tells us about those "in the beginning" days. One of the tasks assigned to Adam was to name the animals. Creative detail at its finest!

The Bible itself contains sixty-six books by more than forty authors and spans more than sixteen hundred years. The Bible is evidence of God's attention to the finite details when you realize it is the inerrant, eternal word of God.

We should not be surprised, then, that when it came time for the God of heaven to have a physical dwelling place on earth, He would be very specific about what that home would be.

The children of Israel had been miraculously delivered from Egyptian captivity. Moses negotiated with Pharaoh – ten plagues worth of back and forth between them. Ultimately, there was the Passover sacrifice and finally the exodus. Exodus 13 and 14 tell us the story of the God-led route they took: "God led them not through the way of the land of the Philistines…but through the way of the wilderness of the Red Sea" (Exodus 13:17-18).

From the beginning of this journey, "The Lord went before them by day in a pillar of cloud, to lead them the way; and by night in a pillar of fire, to give them light; to by day and night" (Exodus 13:21).

That pillar – whether cloud or fire – was always there. In addition to giving them light, perhaps it was also to remind them that Jehovah God was, in fact, leading them every step of their journey. However, they still had their doubts. When the path they traveled led them to the shore of the Red Sea and they found themselves with water in front of them and the armies of Pharaoh in hot pursuit behind them, they had one question for Moses. "Because there were no graves in Egypt, hast thou taken us away to die in the wilderness?" (Exodus 14:11). Moses, their God-called and God-chosen leader had an answer for them:

> "Fear ye not, stand still, and see the salvation of the Lord, which he will shew to you today: for the Egyptians whom ye have seen today, ye shall see them again no more forever. The Lord shall fight for you, and ye shall hold your peace" (Exodus 14:13-14).

The promise of God to Moses was simple:

> "Lift thou up thy rod, and stretch out thine hand
> over the sea, and divide it: and the children of Israel
> shall go on dry ground through the midst of the sea.
> And I, behold, I will harden the hearts of the
> Egyptians, and they shall follow them...And the
> Egyptians shall know that I am the Lord" (Exodus
> 14:16-18).

What a miraculous deliverance was about to occur – that pillar of fire and cloud was going to become the source of light for the children of Israel and simultaneously a source of darkness for Pharaoh's army! Moses stretched out his hand, and the Lord sent a strong east wind that blew all night and dried a pathway through the sea for the children of Israel to march across on dry ground! The Egyptian army continued in hot pursuit, thinking they would follow the children of Israel and capture them when they reached the Red Sea. It was too late to retreat when they realized they had fallen into a trap unlike any other. They were not fighting the devices of men but the God of Israel. There was nothing but defeat in their future.

"Let us flee from the face of Israel; for the Lord fighteth for them against the Egyptians"(Exodus 14:25). They were right; the Jehovah God of Israel was fighting for the children of Israel! The revelation came a little too late. Moses raised his rod again. The sea that parted now returned to itself. "And the waters returned, and covered the chariots, and the horsemen, and all the host of Pharaoh that came into the sea after them; there remained not so much as one of them" (Exodus 14:28).

"Then sang Moses and the children of Israel this
song unto the Lord, and spake, saying, I will sing
unto the Lord, for he hath triumphed gloriously:
the horse and his rider hath he thrown into the sea.
The Lord is my strength and song, and he is
become my salvation: he is my God, and I will
prepare him an habitation" (Exodus 15:1-2).

Their thanksgiving was short-lived and soon replaced by
murmurs and complaints. Despite their freedom from Egyptian
slavery, something in them still longed for some of the benefits of
their bondage. God was providing manna; they craved melons and
cucumbers, leeks and onions. God sent quail. They were not
satisfied. Nothing seemed to be quite enough. Their grumbling
and complaining frustrated Moses and angered Jehovah. Despite
their apparent blessings, it seemed the children of Israel could find
something to gripe about every day. They were buying themselves
forty years of wilderness wandering with their rebellion and
ingratitude.

In time, God summonsed Moses to Mount Sinai with specific
instructions for the rest of the leaders. The elders were to wait at
the foot of the mountain with Aaron and Hur. During this time,
anyone having any kind of need could bring their matters of
importance to these two designees. Exodus 24:15-18 describes the
setting:

"And Moses went up into the mount, and a cloud
covered the mount. And the glory of the Lord
abode upon mount Sinai, and the cloud covered it
six days: and the seventh day he called Moses out of
the midst of the cloud. And the sight of the glory
of the Lord was like devouring fire on the top of the

> mount in the eyes of the children of Israel…And
> Moses was in the mount forty days and forty
> nights."

It was a difficult time for the children of Israel. Their leader was absent. They returned to their pattern of murmuring and complaining. They asked Aaron to make them gods since no one had seen or heard from Moses: "we wot not what is become of him" (Exodus 32:1). Plans were made; jewelry was collected. Too soon they were dancing around worshipping a golden calf.

God was not pleased. He said to Moses:

> "Go, get thee down; for thy people, which thou
> broughtest out of the land of Egypt, have corrupted
> themselves: they have turned aside quickly out of
> the way which I commanded them: they have made
> them a molten calf, and have worshipped it, and
> have sacrificed thereunto, and said, These be thy
> gods, O Israel, which have brought thee up out of
> the land of Egypt" (Exodus 32:7-8).

Moses, coming down from the mountain carrying the stones on which God Himself had written the ten commandments, found Himself angered by the behavior of the Israelites. He flung the tablets from God to the ground, breaking them into pieces that could not be reassembled. Arriving at the foot of the mountain, Moses put the golden calf in the fire, burned it, and then ground it to powder. Moses then added water and forced the children of Israel to drink the tainted and no doubt distasteful water.

Moses set about a path of repentance and restoration for the children of Israel. Among those acts and practices was a tent or tabernacle of meeting. It was at this juncture Moses set up a tent "without the camp." It was here business was conducted among the tribes. It was also a place where "every one which sought the Lord went out unto the tabernacle of the congregation" (Exodus 33:7). This tabernacle or tent – without the camp – pre-dates the tabernacle that was ultimately set up in the wilderness.

Exodus 33:7-10 tells us about this "Tabernacle of the Congregation:"

> "And Moses took the tabernacle, and pitched it without the camp, afar off from the camp, and called it the Tabernacle of the congregation. And it came to pass, that every one which sought the Lord went out unto the tabernacle of the congregation, which was without the camp. And it came to pass, when Moses went out unto the tabernacle, that all the people rose up, and stood every man at his tent door, and looked after Moses, until he was gone into the tabernacle. And it came to pass, as Moses entered into the tabernacle, the cloudy pillar descended, and stood at the door of the tabernacle, and the Lord talked with Moses. And all the people saw the cloudy pillar stand at the tabernacle door: and all the people rose up and worshipped, every man in his tent door."

Moses had a remarkable experience with Jehovah in this tent of congregation, witnessed by the children of Israel prior to his going to Mount Sinai the second time. The Lord had led them from Egypt with that pillar of cloud by day and of fire by night.

On that day, when Moses went into the Tabernacle of the Congregation, the pillar of cloud descended and stood at the door.

The response of the people when they realized the Lord was in the pillar of cloud was to worship: "…all the people rose up and worshipped, every man in his tent door" (Exodus 33:10). It was there "...the Lord spake unto Moses face to face, as a man speaketh unto his friend..." (Exodus 33:11).

Jehovah instructed Moses to re-create the tablets and meet Him on Mount Sinai. It was during this second encounter on Mount Sinai that God gave him the plans for a tabernacle to be built to house His presence in the midst of His people. At the time, the children of Israel were nomads, dwelling in tents. The house for God would also be a tent. It would provide a place for them to offer sacrifices and worship wherever they camped while also being mobile enough to move with them as they journeyed in the desert wilderness.

Jehovah's detailed plan even organized for them exactly how the camp was to be set up, specifying exactly where the tabernacle was to be placed.

Keep in mind this "camp" of the Israelites was comprised of 12 tribes, numbering in total over 603,550 men over the age of 20 and "able to go forth to war" (Numbers 1:45-46). This number did not include women, children, or the disabled. This number also did not include the Levites. The tribe of Levi was responsible for setting up, tearing down, moving, and setting up again the tabernacle tent and all the contents; they were not counted as warriors.

It is estimated by some scholars that the actual number of people in the camp of Israel may have been close to three million or more. When they camped in a particular place, as the resources of that area were depleted, they would break camp and move on to the next location. However, they did not move at the time of their own choosing. Their movements were always directed by the pillar of cloud/fire. When it moved, they followed.

When it came time to establish a tabernacle for His presence on earth, we see again this God of detail. His instructions specified the tabernacle was to be placed in the center of the camp. The Levites were to pitch their tents "round about" the tabernacle (Numbers 1:53). From there, again we read specific instructions of what order and what direction the rest of the tents were to be set up. On the east side was Judah, and next Issachar, and next Zebulun, and on around until the tribes surrounded the tabernacle. Each tribe camped under the standard, or flag, of its patriarch.

Dimensions, materials, purpose and placement were all a part of the instructions given to Moses in seven chapters of the Book of Exodus. From what was to be bronze or brass, to the color of thread to be used on the embroidered curtains, God wanted attention paid to the finite details. He was very explicit in His instructions. All along the way those instructions included specific reminders to follow the plan given and not vary. He is a God of detail; He wanted things done exactly as He planned.

It was to be built with supplies offered from the willing hearts of God's children. God was very specific in His list of needed supplies. Jehovah demanded their best. This Tabernacle of Moses was not going to be built of second-hand materials, nor was it to be assembled by second rate craftsmen.

> "And the Lord spake unto Moses, saying, Speak unto the children of Israel, that they bring me an offering: of every man that giveth it willingly with his heart ye shall take my offering. And this is the offering which ye shall take of them; gold, and

silver, and brass, and blue, and purple, and scarlet,
and fine linen, and goats' hair, And rams' skins
dyed red, and badgers' skins, and shittim wood, oil
for the light, spices for anointing oil, and for sweet
incense, onyx stones, and stones to be set in the
ephod, and in the breastplate" (Exodus 25:1-7).

It was for a single purpose: "And let them make me a
sanctuary; that I may dwell among them" (Exodus 25:8).

It came with a reminder to carefully follow Jehovah God's
explicit instructions. There was to be no variation to the specifics
dictated by God to Moses. There was a pattern for the tabernacle
as a whole, and there was a pattern for each of the instruments that
were to be placed inside it.

> "According to all that I shew thee, after the pattern
> of the tabernacle, and the pattern of all the
> instruments thereof, even so shall ye make it"
> (Exodus 25:9).

It was to be done with excellence by skilled and gifted workers
called by Jehovah and given specific assignments:

> "And Moses said unto the children of Israel, see,
> the Lord hath called by name Bezaleel the son of
> Uri, the son of Hur, of the tribe of Judah; And he
> hath filled him with the spirit of God, in wisdom,
> in understanding, and in knowledge, and in all
> manner of workmanship; And to devise curious
> works, to work in gold, and in silver, and in brass,
> and in the cutting of stones, to set them, and in
> carving of wood, to make any manner of cunning
> work. And he hath put in his heart that he may
> teach, both he, and Aholiab, the son of Ahisamach,

of the tribe of Dan. Them hath he filled with
wisdom of heart, to work all manner of work, of the
engraver, and of the cunning workman, and of the
embroiderer, in blue, and in purple, in scarlet, and
in fine linen, and of the weaver, even of them that
do any work, and of those that devise cunning work.
Then wrought Bezaleel and Aholiab, and every wise
hearted man, in whom the Lord put wisdom and
understanding to know how to work all manner of
work for the service of the sanctuary, according to
all that the Lord had commanded" (Exodus 35:30 –
36:1).

Every dimension, from the spacing of tent posts to the spacing
of the hooks to hang the draperies, was specified. Each piece of
furniture was constructed by following detailed instructions about
size and materials to be used. Very little was left for anyone else to
decide. Every detail and dimension was "according to all that the
Lord had commanded."

The white linen that was used for curtaining the boundaries of
the Outer Court was symbolic of purity and the righteousness of
God. In Revelation 19:8, in the description of the church as the
bride of Christ, we read: "And to her was granted that she should
be arrayed in fine linen, clean and white: for the fine linen is the
righteousness of saints." The priests who served in the tabernacle
were also instructed to wear fine white linen garments when they
entered the service of the Lord (Exodus 28:39-43).

Can you imagine in the drabness of the wilderness desert
what the structure with its bronze and silver-capped pillars looked
like glistening in the morning sun? Can you almost capture the
sound of the white linen draperies that marked the boundaries of
the Outer Court as the desert wind blew through them?

Wooden posts covered with brass and set in sockets of brass designated the boundaries of the Outer Court. The bronze base sockets were symbolic of the judgment of God upon those who sin against Him. The capitals that were atop each of the pillars were made of silver, symbolizing the ransom price God placed on each of the children of Israel. Though the winds of the desert might blow, and though the sands of the desert might shift, these posts in their sockets stood firm. There was no room for a shift in the boundaries established between a holy God and sinful man. The silver hooks and joinings that kept the linen in place between the pillars of wood and brass are significant. Linen, as mentioned earlier, speaks to righteousness. The silver speaks of redemption. Cecil Ducille observed:

> "This plan or pattern contains in symbolic language every iota of God's word, from the Holy Spirit working in the life of the sinner outside of the tent, to bring him in through the gate, to the believer being installed into the Ark of the Covenant in the Holy of Holies with all the attributes of the risen Christ manifested in him" (Cecil J. Ducille, "The Pattern", www.thepatternonline.org).

There were to be two divisions within the tabernacle design: The Outer Court and The Tabernacle of the Congregation. There were then three separate designated areas within the whole.

The Outer Court contained the Brazen Altar and the Laver of Water. Also, placed strategically within the Outer Court was the Tabernacle of Moses. The Holy Place, its entrance marked by Five Pillars, contained the Table of Shewbread, the Golden Candlestick, and the Altar of Incense. The Holy of Holies, separated by a linen veil, contained the Ark of the Covenant, the symbol of the Divine presence of Jehovah.

The Outer Court was rectangular in shape and specified as 100 x 50 cubits. (Based on the 18 inch cubit, this would be 150 x 75 feet.) This Outer Court was enclosed by curtains, 5 cubits in length (7.5 feet) supported by brass pillars. Exodus 27:9-19 tells us the curtains were of "fine twined linen" (v.9) with the pillars and their sockets (bases) made of brass. The fillets (the connecting rod between the pillars) and hooks were of silver. According to the blueprint of God, there were twenty pillars on the north and south, with ten pillars on the east and west. This formed the rectangle shape that would define the Outer Court.

The east side, which included the gate, would have 3 brass pillars and sockets spanning 15 cubits (22.5 feet) on either side of the 20 cubit (30 feet) gate. The linen hanging on the gate was to be "of blue, and purple, and scarlet, and fine twined linen, wrought with needlework" on four brass pillars and sockets (v. 16).

The tabernacle's overall dimensions were 30 x 10 x 10 cubits (45 x 15 x 15 feet) set in the western end of the court. It was obviously - by size, design, and placement - the main feature of the courtyard. The entrance into the Holy Place, like the Outer Court, faced east.

The outer walls of the tabernacle were to be covered by ten curtains of fine twined linen – blue, purple, and scarlet – "…with cherubim of cunning work" (Exodus 26:1). Two sets of five curtains were to be coupled together and then "loops of blue" on the selvedge edge of the coupling – fifty loops to hold them together with taches of gold (Exodus 26:1-6).

At the entrance, there were 5 golden pillars made of acacia wood and overlaid with pure gold, set in sockets of silver. On the interior, the side walls of the tent were made of pillars of acacia wood 15 feet tall and 2.5 feet wide, stood on end, and overlaid in pure gold, bound together with golden bars. They were to be stood in double sockets of silver, with 2 tenons, or stays, for each board.

For the side curtains, there were to be eleven curtains made of goat hair - five curtains coupled together and six curtains coupled together, were to be coupled together – then the two sets of five secured to each other. A specific order was dictated: goats' hair, rams' skins dyed red, and a badger skin covering on top (Exodus 26:13-14). The sides were supported by bars made of acacia wood overlaid with gold, with gold rings to hold them in place.

The front section of this tabernacle was a room, The Holy Place, measuring 20 x 10 cubits (30 x 15 feet), leaving the 10 cubit square remaining for the Holy of Holies. In this room were placed the Table of Shewbread, the Golden Candlestick, and the Altar of Incense. It was here the priests daily came to tend the Candlesticks and to offer morning and evening sacrifices on the Altar of incense. In addition, each Sabbath they placed 12 fresh loaves of bread on the table.

This was a place of separation. The Brazen Altar and the Laver of Water were both out in the open air and could be viewed by those gathered in the courtyard. However, at the door of the tabernacle, the priest set aside his clothing, put on an ephod (a holy garment made of white linen), and entered the Holy Place alone.

In that Holy Place, the priest encountered the Golden Candlestick, the Table of Shewbread, and the Altar of Incense. Each item of furniture was built to Jehovah God's specifications.

Behind the Altar hung the veil that separated the Holy of Holies, created to the exact pattern given by Jehovah:

> "And thou shalt make a vail of blue, and purple,
> and scarlet, and fine twined linen of cunning work:
> with cherubims shall it be made: And thou shalt
> hang it upon four pillars of shittim wood overlaid
> with gold: their hooks shall be of gold, upon the
> four sockets of silver. And thou shalt hang up the
> vail under the taches, that thou mayest bring in
> thither within the vail the ark of the testimony:
> and the vail shall divide unto you between the
> Holy Place and the most holy" (Exodus 26:31-33).

Behind the veil, the Holy of Holies contained a solitary piece of furniture - the Ark of the Covenant. This Holy Place, where the spirit of Jehovah God came down to earth, was a 10 x 10 cubit room. There was no created light in this room, as the curtains banished sunlight. There was no artificial light there either. The only light came when the shekinah presence of God filled the room. In that dark room resided one single piece of furniture. It was not the largest. It was not the tallest. However, it was perhaps the most significant piece of furniture of all. For it was here, when the time came, the Jehovah God of Israel made His presence known in the camp.

The Ark of the Covenant's design was given to Moses with the same attention to detail as every other piece of furniture. This sacred chest was made of acacia wood, covered inside and out with pure gold. It was to measure 2.5 x 1.5 x 1.5 cubits. (This was basically 45 x 27 x 27 inches.) Gold rings were strategically placed to assist in carrying the ark, inserted with wooden poles also covered with gold. Unlike the Brazen Altar, this piece of furniture was a complete box-like structure – with a sealed bottom so it could contain artifacts.

Moses was given special instructions regarding the lid, the Mercy Seat: two hammered gold cherubim (angels) were to face each other, with their wings overshadowing the lid.

> "And there I will meet with thee, and I will commune with thee from above the Mercy Seat, from between the two cherubims which are upon the ark of the testimony, of all things which I will give thee in commandment unto the children of Israel" (Exodus 25:22).

In the wilderness years, the High Priest's duties included annually making atonement for the sins of the children of Israel. Once a year he would go into the Holy of Holies and sprinkle the Mercy Seat with the blood of sacrificed bulls and goats.

At the beginning, the Ark of the Covenant, designed with the angelic beings on its lid, contained only the law: the Ten Commandments Moses had brought down the mountain after his second encounter with Jehovah. We see even then that the God of detail always places mercy above the law. Later a pot of manna was added to the ark as well as Aaron's rod that budded. Each of the contents had its own symbolic meaning. The words of the Law were overshadowed by mercy. The manna was a symbol of God's physical provision for them. Aaron's rod was the symbol of God's authority in the hands of God-chosen men.

Ever present, hovering over this tabernacle, was the pillar of cloud by day and the pillar of fire by night that provided protection and direction to the children of Israel. When it was time for the children of Israel to move to a new location in their wilderness wandering, the pillar would begin to move. While the other tribes packed their tents and belongings and prepared to move, the Levites would carefully pack up the all the furnishings and furniture, the walls, curtains, and gates that comprised this dwelling place of Jehovah God, making special provision to move the Ark of the Covenant.

Countless books have been written by students and scholars on virtually every aspect of this Wilderness Tabernacle. There is a rich world of symbolism to be explored in each detail. The types and shadows of Old Testament to New are present here. Google "The Tabernacle Plan" and related searches, and you'll find innumerable entries and myriad life applications. This particular study is specific to the revolutionary, life-changing power of praying the Tabernacle Plan as it came to and through an anointed minister of the Gospel – my father, G. A. Mangun. Others studied it, preached it, wrote about it long before he did. However, it is what he shared with me - the Purpose, Power, and Pattern of Praying Through The Tabernacle - that became "Heaven to Earth."

CHAPTER TWO

chapter two

PRAYER DOESN'T CHANGE THINGS…
PRAYER CHANGES EVERYTHING

"And the Lord spake unto Moses saying,
'Speak unto the children of Israel,
that they bring me an offering:
of every man that giveth it willingly with his heart
ye shall take my offering…
And let them make me a sanctuary,
that I may dwell among them.
According to all that I shew thee,
after the pattern of the Tabernacle,
and the pattern of all the instruments thereof,
even so shall ye make it."
Exodus 25:1-2, 8-9

"Who serve unto the example and shadow of heavenly things,
as Moses was admonished of God when he was about to make the
Tabernacle: for, see, saith he, that thou make all things
according to the pattern shewed to thee in the mount."
Hebrews 8:5

Before we can embark on any prayer journey, or enter into any study of the tabernacle and tabernacle prayer, we must understand some foundational principles of prayer. These concepts will help us know how to approach God, how to recognize when we are in

His presence, and what to do when we find ourselves there. They will also help us identify what we can expect to receive from God in a place of prayer and intercession.

In Luke 17 and 18, we find Jesus in the midst of a group of scribes and Pharisees, as well as the twelve and other disciples. The Pharisees and scribes were demanding answers to their questions about the kingdom of God and when and how it would come. Ultimately Jesus shared a parable with them.

In the first verse of Luke 18, introducing the parable of the judge and the widow, Jesus gave the only requirement for prayer: "Men ought always to pray." It is something we must simply do and do it always. It is the simplest and most concise instruction.

Jesus also said, "Watch ye therefore, and pray always…" (Luke 21:36). The Apostle Paul reinforces this in I Thessalonians 5:17: "Pray without ceasing."

Thousands of years earlier, when God gave Moses the pattern for the Tabernacle of Moses, He revealed not just the details of a physical Tabernacle in the Wilderness for the children of Israel, but the pattern and purpose for prayer.

God established a tabernacle through His servant, Moses, so the Israelites could understand how to come into His presence. Through the design of that tabernacle, God illustrated what is required in order to be able to stand in His presence. That tabernacle demonstrates the attributes of God and shows us how His blessings are made accessible to His people. The Tabernacle of Moses, with explicit instructions for all aspects of its construction from dimensions to design to construction materials and placement, was for the sole purpose of providing a place where God could commune with His children. Exodus 25:21-22 states clearly this intended purpose of the Holy of Holies and the importance of our being in that place: "And there I will meet with thee, and I will commune with thee from above the Mercy Seat, from between the two cherubims which are upon the ark of the testimony, of all things which I will give thee in commandment unto the children of Israel." It is a meeting place, a place of communion, a place of commitment and commandment. It is the Holy of Holies.

As we progress through this book, we will study each aspect of the tabernacle. The details of each piece of furniture and both its intended use and symbolic meaning will be shared. This will help us use the Tabernacle Plan of prayer to establish a new dimension of powerful prayer in our lives. As we become familiar with it, we will be able to pray according to that God-given pattern wherever we are: at home, at the office, in the car, or in a prayer room.

Prayer brings to us – and develops within us – divine inner strength. Without the presence of God residing in our lives, we have no recourse other than to respond to external pressures and temptations from without. Doing this will leave us weak and failing in our walk with God, falling apart in a crisis, and eventually giving up. This is not the plan or will of God and is not the will of God for our lives. He wants us prayerfully strong.

The strength of our prayer lives – the tabernacle of prayer we build into our everyday existences – will determine our response to the outer things of life. If we have God's presence inside, nothing that comes against us from the outside will be able to overcome us.

"Greater is he that is in you than he that is in the world" (I John 4:4).

God designed that first tabernacle to be portable. As they moved around the wilderness, He gave instructions for taking it down, for picking up, and for transporting the pieces. There were exact instructions for moving not just the walls and the linens but every piece of furniture from one place to the next. It is hard for us to understand that literally every piece of that structure was sanctified and sacred. The Israelites knew it and respected it. They understood that if they kept God's tabernacle in order, the presence of the Lord would continue to lead them. The fire by night and the pillar by day would continue to radiate light and direction to them. They understood that every part of the tabernacle, from the Entrance Gate to the Ark of the Covenant, had to be in order. No matter where their journey took them, when the tabernacle was set up, it had to be done in careful and precise order.

The tabernacle held the very presence of the Jehovah God of Israel. It was the first time in human history that God had come down and actually dwelt among His people. They understood that if even one element was out of place, His presence could be affected. They knew that if they did not pay careful attention to the smallest of details they had been given, this wonderful new relationship with God might be broken.

The children of Israel would not wander in the wilderness always. However, God Jehovah would visit them in this designated Holy Place as they moved from place to place because, with each move, they were ever coming closer to God's ultimate purpose for them. Today, we must understand there is no longer a physical place where the holy presence of God dwells. We are that place, and He desires to commune with us "ever' day."

Just as there were specific instructions and a divine order to the tabernacle, we must have lives we willingly live according to the pattern He has given us. In I Corinthians 6:19, Paul said, "Know ye not that your body is the temple of the Holy Ghost..." We are His temple – His dwelling place - in the world today. As the temple of the Holy Spirit, we must handle carefully the sacred pieces that we house. We must be careful not to do anything that would adversely affect those pieces. It is not the external things people say about us that are important – nor the things people may have done to us that truly matter. Our relationship with God is determined by how we handle – or mishandle – that internal tabernacle of the one true and living God.

This study of "Heaven to Earth" puts responsibility for our relationship with God where He has placed it: on us! If we have a true desire to know God, to be His chosen vessel, this prayer plan will revolutionize our lives, our thinking, and our praying. Our lives will become lives of prayer. We may be surrounded by external problems; yet, through this God-given pattern of prayer, we can rise above every one of them. Once we establish this heavenly relationship with God and sanctify it (set it apart and protect it), we will be able to handle anything that comes.

My father used this pattern of "Praying through the Tabernacle" in his personal prayer life for close to seven decades. Following his death in 2010, when I first started my in-depth study of his private and personal notes on the subject, an illustration came to mind.

Though I have never had a custom-made suit, I have had the opportunity to have a shirt made-to-order. When one goes to the tailor, the first thing he does is take measurements. From the individual measurements, a pattern is created. Then, the tailor lays that pattern on the selected fabric and cuts the pattern. If he cuts without the pattern, the garment won't fit. If he ignores the pattern and cuts a little wider there and a little shorter here, there will be a few problems. The finished product may still be beautiful to behold; however, if the tailor cut the sleeves 2 inches shorter than the pattern, the shirt cannot be worn.

The same is true with God's presence. He has given us a pattern to follow. If we deviate from the pattern, we will come up short and not come into the fullness of His presence that He desires for us. God told Moses, "…see…that thou make all things according to the pattern shewed to thee in the mount" (Exodus 25:40). The measurements and patterns for the tabernacle in the Old Testament were very important to God.

The pattern of prayer set forth in this book will help us understand that when we enter into a life of prayer, God does not want us to wander aimlessly in the realm of the Spirit. He wants us to know exactly where He is so we can come into His presence, follow His pattern, and find "fullness of joy and pleasures for evermore" (Psalm 16:11).

When we pray according to the pattern, God is faithful and just to hear and answer us. I John 5:14-15 says,

> "And this is the confidence that we have in him, that, if we ask any thing according to his will, he heareth us: And if we know that he hear us, whatsoever we ask, we know that we have the petitions we desired of him."

When we pray, as long as we keep our focus on Him and seek His counsel and His will, rather than our own, we have His promise:

> "So shall my word be that goeth forth out of my
> mouth: it shall not return unto me void, but it shall
> accomplish that which I please, and it shall
> prosper *in the thing* whereto I sent it" (Isaiah 55:11).

As we pray we can know God is merciful and acts according to His will. By looking for God's pattern in our prayer lives, we come into a fullness of prayer and relationship with Him. This prayer pattern, because of its effectiveness, will bring you to a consistent time and place of prayer. It will bring you a new confidence in prayer. As we spend time in His presence, we come to know Him; His plans and purposes become clear. While we may not have a visible evidence of the presence of God at work in our lives like the pillar of fire and cloud, we will know the journey of our lives is under His direction just as much as their journey in the wilderness was directed by Him.

May the God of the ages commune with us, His children, from the Mercy Seat, answering our prayers, providing counsel and comfort to our hearts – as he did Moses at the time of the dedication of the Tabernacle in the Wilderness:

> "And when Moses was gone into the tabernacle of
> the congregation to speak with him, then he heard
> the voice of one speaking unto him
> from off the Mercy Seat that was upon the ark of
> testimony, from between the two cherubims: and he
> spake unto him" (Numbers 7:89).

CHAPTER THREE

chapter three

The Tabernacle in the Wilderness
The Cross At Calvary
Shadows, Symbols, and Signs

Through the years various individuals, prayerful men and women, Bible scholars and skilled theologians, have linked the symbolisms, types, and shadows of the Tabernacle in the Wilderness to the cross at Calvary. Whether studied in depth or just for a surface analysis, the connection between the Old Testament and the New, the story of redemption for the Children of Israel and redemption once and for all for humankind on Calvary is there.

The first place we see a glimpse of the cross is in the instructions given Moses for the way the tents of the tribes of Israel were to be set up around the tabernacle. With the tabernacle in the center and the Entrance Gate facing east, directions were given for tents of the various tribes to be set up. This divine design for the campsite of the children of Israel formed a cross.

The instructions for the specific placement of the tents and tribes was as detailed as the plans given for building the Outer Court, the Tabernacle of Moses, and all its fixtures. God's orders were clear, concise, and not to be manipulated. God had a plan. He is a God of detail. His plan was, therefore, very specific and precise.

God was paying attention and knew that only if they did as He said would He be able to come to earth and dwell with them. It was important to Him.

The tabernacle and the tents of the Levites were in the center, to be set up first. The tribe of Levi was not numbered but set up around all sides of the tabernacle.

> "But the Levites were not numbered among the children of Israel; as the Lord commanded Moses. And the children of Israel did according to all that the Lord commanded Moses: so they pitched by their standards, and so they set forward, every one after their families, according to the house of their fathers" (Numbers 2:33-34).

Set up to the east was the camp of Judah. This was made up of three tribes: Judah, Issachar, and Zebulun. This group totaled 186,400 men (Numbers 2:3-7).

To the south was the encampment of Reuben, consisting of the tribes of Rueben, Simeon, and Gad. This group totaled 151,450 men (Number 2:8-17).

The camp of Ephraim, made up of the tribes of Ephraim, Manasseh, and Benjamin, totaled 108,100 men and was camped to the west (Number 2:18-24).

To to the north was the camp of Dan. This group consisted of the tribes of Dan, Asher, and Naphtali and totaled approximately 157,600 men (Numbers 2:25-31).

Can you even imagine trying to get all of those people with supplies, animals, children, and wives organized and moved from one place to another? If you've ever relocated a family of four or more from one house to another, pets and all, you might have an inkling of what went on every time the children of Israel moved through the wilderness. Except, you didn't have the added pleasure of coordinating your move with thousands of other families and all of their stuff.

Number 2:2 shares this instruction regarding setting up the camp: "Every man of the children of Israel shall pitch by his own standard, with the ensign of their father's house: far off about the tabernacle of the congregation shall they pitch."

The word used in the phrase "by his own standard" is a Hebrew word that means "to put up the flag" and is often used in reference to a "troop with banners." These "standards" provided a visual symbol to identify rallying points for the children of Israel whether they were camped or traveling. The "ensign" is from a word that means "look, behold." These ensigns "of their father's house" identified the households within the troops. Both types of flags uniquely identified each tribe and each family within each tribe.

One commentary shared the following observation:

"In order for the camps to be differentiated, such standards would necessarily differ in color, insignia or both. Since the tabernacle was quite small, it seems impractical for the four cardinal directions to have been restricted in width by the dimensions of the tabernacle itself. It seems likely that the Levites, who were not numbered, camped around the tabernacle equally in all four directions and then the other four camps extended outward from there. Given Levitical attention to detail, whoever camped outside of the clear directions of east, south, west, and north (e.g., northwest) would be violating these directional instructions (e.g., by being both north and west). Using the populations given for the four camps, the ratios of their relative sizes would have been: Judah (1.0); Reuben (0.81); Ephraim (0.58); and Dan (0.85). Assuming the Levites encamped in a square and a uniform width for each camp extending strictly outward in the four cardinal directions, the view from above, as Balaam saw it (Numbers 23:9) may have resembled a cross" (Garland, Tony, A Testimony of Christ, A Commentary on the Book of Revelation. 7.2 Camp of Israel, www.biblestudytools.com).

To be noted, is the school of thought that the pieces of furniture and the layout of the tabernacle also has rich symbolism to connect it to Christ and His sacrifice for us.

The Brazen Altar, the first and largest piece of furniture encountered in that wilderness dwelling place, was a symbol of the cross of Christ. Jesus Christ was our perfect Lamb of God. When He died, He did it once and for all. Our sins were paid in full. No longer would the blood of animals be required.

We next encounter the Laver of Water, used for ceremonial cleansing. We know water cannot wash away our sin. The blood of Jesus does that. However, it does something else as well. It brings with it new life. This Laver of Water is where new life begins. As one commentator observed, "It is not merely washing away the old, but rather a completely new creation" (https://bible.org/seriespage/8-tabernacle-picture-jesus-exodus-25-30\).

This washing is symbolic of New Testament water baptism as practiced in the Book of Acts.

Step into the Holy Place where the Golden Candlestick was housed, and encounter Jesus Christ the light of the World. Approach the Table of Bread, and find "the Bread of Life," a title Jesus gave Himself in John 6:48. Come to the Altar of Incense where the smell of incense burning becomes the scent and symbol of our prayer. These three items become the cross beam of the cross. The place of the oil of His presence, the Altar where incense of praise and worship is offered, and the table where there is bread that is sustenance for life's journey become the place that bore the weight of His broken body.

From that center-set Altar of Incense, we step beyond the veil into the Holy of Holies where the shekinah presence of God can be found with the Ark of the Covenant. Fire from the Brazen Altar is brought into this place. Blood is applied to the cherubs on the top of the Ark. Mercy is above the law. There, His presence is felt. The truest of communion between God and man occurs. There, in that worship and communion with God, the work of the cross of Christ is complete.

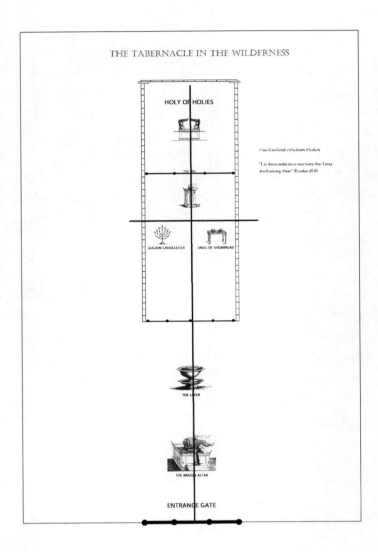

This is the diagram Bishop G. A. Mangun used to show the pattern of the cross as it fits the diagram of the Tabernacle of Moses in the wilderness.

CHAPTER FOUR

THE ENTRANCE GATE
The Only Way

*"And for the gate of the court shall be an hanging of twenty cubits,
of blue, and purple, and scarlet, and fine twined linen,
wrought with needlework:
and their pillars shall be four, and their sockets four."*
Exodus 27:16

*"Enter into his gates with thanksgiving,
and into his courts with praise:
be thankful unto him, and bless his name."*
Psalm 100:4

"I am the way and the truth and the life..."
John 14:6

chapter 4

THE ENTRANCE GATE
The Only Way

As detailed and specific as the instructions were for every aspect of the Tabernacle in the Wilderness, the placement and measurement of the Entrance Gate was no exception.

This singular entrance was a specific size: 20 cubits. The linen was to be of a specific color and design: blue, purple, and scarlet needlework on fine twined white linen. The gate was to have four pillars and four sockets.

Jehovah God even specified that this gate was to be placed where it faced east. Whenever they moved, wherever they moved, putting this Entrance in the right position, facing the right direction was the first step in setting the rest of the tabernacle, as well as the rest of the camp of the Israelites, in place.

This beautiful segment of an otherwise plain wall would not only designate it as the gate of entrance, but provide a beautiful and colorful place spotlighted by the light of the rising sun to welcome people to this place of worship.

The dimensions of the full enclosure of the Outer Court were 100 x 50 cubits, a rectangle formed by a series of pillars and linen hangings. This "wall" was to be 5 cubits in height. The gate itself was to be 20 cubits, placed in the center of the 50 cubit side.

There is no way for us today to know the exact measure of a Biblical cubit. In Bible times, a cubit was determined by the measurement from a man's elbow to his fingertips. Obviously, this was not a very precise measurement and could vary anywhere from 17.5 inches to 20.6 inches (How Long Was the Original Cubit? by Bodie Hodge on April 1, 2007 - answersingenesis.org/noahs-ark/how-long-was-the-original-cubit/-).

Utilizing a website called convertingunits.com, and a little of today's math, we can approximate that the total enclosure was almost 50 x 25 yards. The gate was almost 10 yards wide. The 5-cubit-height translates to just over 7 feet: 7.3818897637795 to be exact.

It must be duly noted there was only one entrance into the Outer Court. You could walk the perimeter of the enclosure, and nowhere along the 100 cubit north and south walls, nor anywhere on the 50 cubit west wall, was an entrance or exit to the Outer Court. You could not get into the Outer Court, nor gain entrance to the tabernacle itself, without going through this designated Entrance Gate. Whether you were a common Jew or a priest, rich man or pauper, this one entrance was your only entrance to the place of sacrifice and worship.

The gate is that "type and shadow" of Jesus Christ who would thousands of years later proclaim, "I am the way . . ." (John 14:6) and "I am the door..." (John 10:9) and "...no man cometh unto the Father but by me..." (John 14:6). He is the one and only God incarnate. It is only by Him and through Him that we gain entrance into this place of worship and redemption.

THE PURPOSE, POWER, AND PATTERN

The Purpose of the Old Testament Wilderness Tabernacle had three distinct focuses. First, and primarily, the tabernacle gave the children of Israel a much-needed physical symbol of God's presence in their midst. In their world, many peoples worshipped other gods as idols that were affixed in their homes and at very public pagan Altars. This tabernacle gave their Jehovah God a dwelling place that was unlike any other. Unlike those other gods, Jehovah God desired for Himself a place to dwell among His children. In Exodus 28:8 we read God's spoken purpose for the tabernacle as given to Moses: "…that I may dwell among them." It was to be His dwelling place, His sanctuary, a place set apart for Him to commune with His chosen people.

Secondly, the tabernacle was a type and shadow of Jesus Christ fulfilling the law. It was a physical foretelling of the "lamb slain from the foundation" (Revelation 13:8). What was, in fact, was about what was to come.

> "Moreover he sprinkled with blood both the tabernacle, and all the vessels of the ministry. And almost all things are by the law purged with blood; and without shedding of blood is no remission. *It was* therefore necessary that the patterns of things in the heavens should be purified with these; but the heavenly things themselves with better sacrifices than these. For Christ is not entered into the Holy Places made with hands, *which are* the figures of the true; but into heaven itself, now to appear in the presence of God for us: Nor yet that he should offer himself often, as the high priest entereth into the Holy Place every year with blood of others; For

then must he often have suffered since the
foundation of the world: but now once in the end of
the world hath he appeared to put away sin by the
sacrifice of himself" (Hebrews 9:22-26).

And, last but not least, the Tabernacle of Moses demonstrated
the divine process by which sinful man could approach a holy God.
Sin would not have the final say. Ultimately, the relationship
between man and God that was broken by sin could be, and would
be, restored through Jesus Christ.

The fine white linen curtains that marked the perimeter of the
Outer Court are indicative of the sinless life of Jesus Christ and
speak of His righteousness. Man's lack of righteousness keeps
Him from the presence of God. Thus, these pure white linen
curtains were what stood between sinful man and righteous God.
The purity of God reflected in the drapery that marked the outside
curtains and formed the wall around the Outer Court.

However, there was a Gate. Entrance into the Court and
access to the God of all ages was not impossible. The Entrance
Gate – like Jesus Christ Himself – allows us access to the presence
of Almighty God.

The colors of the needlework and linen at the gate each had
their own significance. Blue, purple and scarlet were specifically
dictated by God to Moses and implicitly followed in preparing the
place where Jehovah God would dwell.

Blue references the divinity of Christ and the color of heaven.
The type and shadow here is of the fact the God of heaven veiled
Himself in human flesh and lived among men. It is what the

Scripture refers to as the great mystery of godliness that "…God was manifest in the flesh, justified in the Spirit, seen of angels, preached unto the Gentiles, believed on in the world, received up into glory" (I Timothy 3:16).

Purple is the color of royalty in Scripture. In Judges 8:26 we read of: "…purple raiment that was on the kings of Midian." It is here we see the power, majesty, and dignity of Jesus Christ our King. It reminds us of the promised day when "The kingdoms of this world are become the kingdoms of our Lord, and of his Christ; and he shall reign for ever and ever" (Revelation 11:15).

Scarlet, the color of blood, speaks to the sacrifice of Jesus Christ the spotless Lamb. There is no way to measure the amount of blood that was shed in the offering of bulls and goats through the centuries. Blood was, from the beginning a part of the plan of redemption. The Lamb was slain from the foundation of the earth (Revelation 13:8). Blood would be shed at the Tabernacle of Moses. Yet, someday at Calvary, the blood of Jesus Christ, the spotless Lamb of God, would put an end to the need for blood sacrifices.

I Peter 1:18-21 tells us of that sacrifice and its purpose and power:

> "Forasmuch as ye know that ye were not redeemed with corruptible things, as silver and gold, from your vain conversation received by tradition from your fathers; But with the precious blood of Christ, as of a lamb without blemish and without spot: Who verily was foreordained before the foundation of the world, but was manifest in these last times for you, who by him do believe in God, that raised him

up from the dead, and gave him glory; that your faith and hope might be in God."

These four columns represent Christ Himself. First as "the door" and "the way" - the only way for sinful man to access a holy God. They are also representative of the four Gospels, the writings of the men who tell His story: Matthew, Mark, Luke, and John.

Matthew's Gospel shares Christ as King with us, the son of David, the descendant of Abraham. Mark portrays Him as the faithful servant of God. Luke, the physician, reveals Christ's humanity, labeling Him the "Son of man." John, in his writing, reveals Jesus Christ to be the "Son of God." These four gospels are the books that tell the story of Jesus.

These four strategically placed pillars are a reminder to us, as we enter into a place of communion and worship that becomes the first steps of our journey to the shekinah presence of God, that Jesus Christ Himself is the only way by which we now access the God of glory. Jesus Christ – that One in whom "dwells all the fullness of the Godhead bodily" (Colossians 2:9) and that God-man who proclaimed, "I and my Father are one" (John 10:30) - is the only way humankind can access the glory and presence of God today.

Special Note: *We will encounter four columns further into the Tabernacle Plan. However, this first Entrance Gate – created by four columns – designating this place of declared praise and heart-felt worship is our entrance into Praying the Tabernacle.*

Jesus spoke of a "strait gate" and noted, "…strait is the gate, and narrow is the way, which leadeth unto life" (Matthew 7:14).

Almighty God incarnated Himself in flesh and, according to Philippians 2:7-8, "took upon him the form of a servant, and was made in the likeness of men: and being found in fashion as a man, he humbled himself, and became obedient unto death, even the death of the cross."

So it is, that Jesus is, indeed, the only entrance. Hebrews 11:6 tells us, "...for he that cometh to God must believe that he is, and that he is a rewarder of them that diligently seek him." We must believe that He is. We must believe that, as we seek Him in prayer, He will hear and answer and reward.

The Power of praise and worship is immeasurable. It brings soothing comfort to the troubled mind and heart. It brings rest to the weary. It brings hope to the struggling. It brings hope to the hopeless and direction to the wandering. Praise is one of the most powerful forces in the world.

The instruction from the Psalmist David is simple. It is with thanksgiving and praise we gain entrance through the gate and find a place in His courts. With the Tabernacle Prayer Plan we begin our journey of "praying through the tabernacle." We enter with words of thanksgiving and praise spoken not just with our lips but from our hearts.

Lauren Daigle, a popular Christian artist, wrote a lyric that comes to mind in conveying the concept of praise and thanksgiving being the first prayers prayed and first words spoken.

"Before I bring my need I will bring my heart
Before I lift my cares I will lift my arms
I wanna know You, I wanna find You
In every season, In every moment

Before I bring my need, I will bring my heart
And seek You first
(Daigle, Lauren. *First.* On *How Can It Be.*
Centric Songs, 2015. Centricity, 2015)."

The Pattern begins here with a simple first step. We enter into His presence – into the Outer Court of the tabernacle – when we walk through the Entrance Gate with words of praise. We have sins for which we must repent. We have needs we are compelled to bring to Him. We have sacrifices that must be offered. We want so much from Him. However, before any of these things, before anything else, we must lift our voices in praise and thanksgiving for who He is and what He has already done.

We proclaim His greatness and thank Him for His glorious acts. It is here we can read and reflect on the words of praise found in the Psalms. It is here we cry, "Bless the Lord, O my soul: and all that is within me..." (Psalm 103:1).

We can join the Psalmist in declaring:

"Open to me the gates of righteousness: I will go
into them, and I will praise the Lord: This gate of
the Lord, into which the righteous shall enter. I will
praise thee: for thou hast heard me, and art become
my salvation" (Psalm 118:19-21).

To put the Entrance Gate instruction into the simplest vernacular of our day, I share Psalm 100:4 from *The Message*:

Enter with the password: "Thank you!"
Make yourselves at home, talking praise
Thank him. Worship him.

CHAPTER FIVE

THE BRAZEN ALTAR
The Place of Sacrifice and Repentance

"And thou shalt make an altar of shittim wood,
five cubits long, and five cubits broad; the altar shall be foursquare:
and the height thereof shall be three cubits.
And thou shalt make the horns of it upon the four corners thereof:
his horns shall be of the same: and thou shalt overlay it with brass.
And thou shalt make his pans to receive his ashes,
and his shovels, and his basons, and his fleshhooks, and his firepans:
all the vessels thereof thou shalt make of brass.
And thou shalt make for it a grate of network of brass;
and upon the net shalt thou make four brasen rings
in the four corners thereof.
And thou shalt put it under the compass of the altar beneath,
that the net may be even to the midst of the altar.
And thou shalt make staves for the altar, staves of shittim wood,
and overlay them with brass.
And the staves shall be put into the rings,
and the staves shall be upon the two sides of the altar, to bear it.
Hollow with boards shalt thou make it:
as it was shewed thee in the mount, so shall they make it."
Exodus 27:1-8

chapter five

THE BRAZEN ALTAR
The Place of Sacrifice and Repentance

The Brazen Altar was the first piece of furniture the children of Israel encountered after entering through the Gate. It was made of acacia wood, overlaid with brass. The dimensions were specified 5 x 5 x 3 cubits (7.38 x 7.38 x 4.43 feet).

The plans were given for exactly how the Brazen Altar was to be constructed along with the instruments needed to facilitate the sacrifice to be in place; all were to be made of brass. Rings and staves were to be in place for when the time came to move the Altar – carved of shittim (acacia) wood and overlaid with brass. Every precise detail was given to Moses with the instruction "As it was shewed thee in the mount, so shall they make it" (Exodus 27:8). And so it was that when all was done and the Tabernacle in the Wilderness consecrated to the Lord Most High that it was written, "Thus did Moses: according to all that the Lord commanded him, so did he" (Exodus 40:16).

The 5 cubit square was hollow; it had no bottom structure. Halfway down, there was a mesh grate on which the wood sat for the burning of sacrifices. Under the grate was built up earth on which the entire Altar rested, setting it above the rest of the courtyard.

Placed on each of the four corners of the structure were triangular additions in a horn shape. These horns were to help in securing the animal sacrifices to the Altar. In Exodus 29, when instructions were given for the sin offering of a bullock, Aaron and his sons were to put the blood on the horns of the Altar with their finger, then pour the remaining blood on the ground beside the bottom of the Altar.

The Psalmist referred to the horns of the Altar when he wrote, "...bind the sacrifice with cords, even unto the horns of the Altar." The horns of the Altar would later provide a place of asylum and safety for the innocent accused of a crime. (You can read the story of Adonijah and Solomon in the first chapter of I Kings and see how Adonijah "...caught hold on the horns of the Altar.")

There were rings set on two opposite sides of the Altar, through which poles could be placed for carrying it. These poles were also made of acacia wood and covered with brass.

A Little About Altars

Prior to this setting, altars had been built by different men in different settings with different materials. In the Book of Genesis, we find altars built by the patriarchs of old.

The word "altar" appears 434 times the King James text. The Hebrew word for altar, mizbeach (miz-bay'-akh), a noun, comes from the root word zabach (zaw-backh), a verb that means "to slaughter for sacrifice." This action-based root word indicates that the altar was, at its core, a physical place just inside the gate of the Outer Court that was intended for sacrificial action. It was constructed of wood and overlaid with brass.

Though there might well have been altars built before then, the first mention of an altar is with Noah, in Genesis 8:20, when he built an altar after the waters of the Great Flood receded. Abraham built an altar when he received the promise from God, "Unto thy seed will I give this land" and again on the mountain where he called upon the name of the Lord (Genesis 12:7-8).

In Genesis 13:18, Abraham built another altar when he came to dwell in the plain of Mamre, in Hebron. Abraham built an altar in Genesis 22 on Mount Moriah on which he sacrificed a ram, though he had been willing to sacrifice his son.

Isaac built an altar when the Lord appeared to him in Genesis 26 at Beersheba after re-digging the wells of Abraham. It was the place where he "called upon the name of the Lord" (Genesis 26:25).

Jacob built an altar at Shalem, where he bought a parcel of land and pitched his tent. He called the place El-elohe-Israel. Then he built another altar at Bethel saying, "I will make there an altar unto God, who answered me in the day of my distress, and was with me in the way which I went" (Genesis 35:3), calling the place El-Bethel because it was there God had appeared to him (Genesis 35:7).

These altars were built of dirt and stone. They were meant to stand in a particular place and commemorate a specific time and event. They were not portable. They were never meant to be movable. They were to stand as memorials to all who saw them to mark a place where God visited mankind.

The Altar built by God's instruction for the Tabernacle of Moses was the first piece of furniture in God's plan of bringing sinful man into a place of righteousness, of giving the unrighteous a means by which to access the righteousness of God.

The Brazen Altar demonstrated to the Israelites – and demonstrates to us today – that the first step for sinful man to approach a holy God is for there to be a cleansing by the blood of an innocent creature. Here we see the type and shadow of the death of Jesus Christ as our blood sacrifice. As the Israelites were compelled to offer an animal without blemish or defect, so Jesus Christ offered Himself, a spotless sinless Lamb.

When we study the Brazen Altar in the plan of God for that first dwelling place in the wilderness, we see, too, the cross of Christ – Jesus Christ and Him crucified – lifted up from the earth, a sacrifice for all. There were cords on the Altar to bind the sacrifice there; there were nails in Jesus's hands and feet to hold Him to the cross. However, what truly kept Him there was His everlasting love for us. "Greater love hath no man than this, that a man lay down his life for his friends . . ." (John 15:13).

The Sacrifices

When the tabernacle was dedicated to God, by Moses, Aaron, and his sons, specific instructions were again given by God and followed by man. From the beginning, God's plan for the redemption of man required blood. Jesus was referred to as "the Lamb slain from the foundation of the world" in Revelation 13:8. We see it in Genesis, when animals were slain to provide skins for Adam and Eve to cover themselves. We see it with Cain and Abel when one sacrifice was accepted and another was not.

Leviticus 17:11 explains:

> "For the life of the flesh is in the blood; and I have given it to you upon the Altar to make an atonement for your souls; for it is the blood that maketh an atonement for the soul."

In I Peter 1:18-19 we read:

> "Forasmuch as ye know that ye were not redeemed with corruptible things, as silver and gold, from your vain conversation received by tradition from your fathers; But with the precious blood of Christ, as of a lamb without blemish and without spot:"

The Law given to Moses was very specific about sacrificial offerings. There were voluntary offerings and mandatory offerings with instructions given for each. There were three types of voluntary offerings: the burnt offering, the grain offering, and the peace offering. The mandatory offerings were the sin offering and the trespass offering.

The voluntary burnt offering was where the individual could offer a burnt offering as an act of worship to express their commitment and devotion to Jehovah God. This type of sacrifice also covered one's unintentional sins. The offering could be a bull a bird (specifically, a turtle dove), or a ram – all without blemishes.

There was a grain offering which was accompanied by a drink offering. Fruit of the field, baked bread made of grain, fine flour and oil with salt were included here. The drink offering, usually an amount of wine equivalent to about one quart, was poured into the fire of the Altar. This offering was to express thanksgiving to God, recognizing that His provision to the person offering the sacrifice.

The peace offering was the third type of voluntary offering and could consist of offering any unblemished animal and/or various grains and breads. This was considered another sacrifice of thanksgiving.

The sin offering was for atonement and purification. The Law offered five possible elements: a young bull, a male goat, a female goat, a doe/pigeon, or 1/10 ephah of fine flower. The type of animal was determined by the individual's financial situation. Specific and detailed instructions were given to the process of sacrifice.

The trespass offering, also a mandatory sacrifice, was exclusively a ram. It was intended to provide cleansing from defiling sins and atonement for unintentional sins that required some kind of restitution or reimbursement to an offended party.

Each of these sacrifices detailed by the Law were, in fact, pointing us toward Jesus Christ, the perfect and final sacrifice for us all. Hebrews 10:10 reminds us that the death of Jesus Christ – the Lamb of God slain for us all – was enough to sanctify all of us: "By the which will we are sanctified through the offering of the body of Jesus Christ once *for all*" (italics added). It is here, at the Brazen Altar, we offer ourselves to Him.

THE PURPOSE, POWER, AND PATTERN

The Purpose of the Brazen Altar, that first stopping place inside the court, was to be a place of sacrifice and redemption. It was the place where the price for sin was paid. The fact that Jesus died once and for all eliminated any further need for the blood of bulls and goats. However, it did not eliminate the daily need for us to have repentant hearts and live repentant lives.

Having entered into the court with our words and songs of thanksgiving and praise, we find ourselves face to face with the Altar. It is a place where we must humble ourselves and admit our need for Jesus Christ. He cannot save us if we think we are not in need of saving. He cannot redeem us if we don't bring to Him our need for redemption.

This is the place where we repent before God for the sin in our lives and heart and minds. There are sins of omission as well as sins of commission. There are secret sins and public sins. Like Paul, we acknowledge "For the good that I would I do not: but the evil which I would not, that I do. Now if I do that I would not, it is no more I that do it, but sin that dwelleth in me" (Romans 7:19).

The Power of the Brazen Altar, the place of repentance that follows our time of praise, is that it is where we are reminded of a simple truth captured in the words of the prophet Isaiah: "All we like sheep have gone astray; we have turned every one to his own way" (Isaiah 53:6).

It is at this Brazen Altar that every one of us come face to face with our sinfulness and His holiness. We are all sinners in need of a Savior. Jesus Christ Himself serves as our priest, and at the Brazen Altar He accepts the sacrifices we offer Him. He hears our prayers of repentance and forgives. He applies His blood and redeems our sin.

We must understand the imperative of prayerful repentance. The honesty and depth of our repentance at the Brazen Altar affects, ultimately, our access to the power of God's presence when we approach the Ark of the Covenant in the Holy of Holies. The

Psalmist understood the principle of repentance being integral to communication with God:

> "If I regard iniquity in my heart, the Lord will not hear me: But verily God hath heard me; he hath attended to the voice of my prayer. Blessed be God, which hath not turned away my prayer, nor his mercy from me" (Psalm 66:18-20).

As we study the different pieces of furniture that were placed in this wilderness dwelling place for the God of Israel, it must be noted that the Brazen Altar was larger than any of the other six pieces of furniture. In fact, all of the other pieces of furniture could fit inside the dimensions of that Altar. We live in a world in which commitment is a disappearing art. It is a world where people seem to seek after small Altars and oversize arks. Yet, in reality, God's plan for all of us is for there to be big Altars for our repentance and for the place of communion – the ark – to be a place of intimacy rather than one of grandeur. As your altar of sacrifice becomes bigger, you find yourself ever more intimate in your personal encounters with our holy God.

No person, place, or thing is too large to be placed on this Altar. There is no sin that He cannot forgive, no situation He cannot redeem. You might think your sins are greater than anyone else's, that your lifetime sin achievement is so high and deep and wide that it cannot possibly be washed away. Yet, I Peter 2:24 tells us He bore all of our sins "in his own body on the tree." Isaiah 53:5-6 assures us:

> "But he was wounded for our transgressions, he was bruised for our iniquities: the chastisement of our peace was upon him; and with his stripes we are

healed. All we like sheep have gone astray; we have turned every one to his own way; and the Lord hath laid on him the iniquity of us all."

"The iniquity of us all" does not allow for exceptions.

Not only was this massive Altar the largest piece of furniture, it was the most frequently used item. It was only once a year that the high priest went into the Holy of Holies. At morning and evening, the other priests would enter the Holy Place. But every day, throughout the day, people could come to offer their sacrifices to Jehovah.

The Pattern of Tabernacle Prayer brings us to this Brazen Altar to create a space in our own lives for daily repentance. Seeking God for the power of His blood to redeem us from the sins of human life must become a part of our Christian walk as we bring our faults and failures to Him.

Jesus Christ – God incarnate – the Word made flesh – made a choice. He said, "No man taketh it from me, but I lay it down of myself. I have power to lay it down, and I have power to take it again" (John 10:18). The very ones who just hours before had been crying in the streets of Jerusalem, "Blessed is he that comes in the name of the Lord," cried out, "Crucify Him!" He made the choice to lay Himself on the cross of Calvary in order to redeem you and me. We must make the choice to lay ourselves on the Brazen Altar of sacrifice and allow His blood to cover us and redeem us.

BibleHistory.com observed,

> "He chose to go to the place of total abandonment and humiliation and become a sin offering, the very object of all of God's wrath . . . so that He could

win for Himself a bride, and pay the debt in full"
(https://www.biblehistory.com/tabernacle/TAB4
The_Bronze_Altar.htm).

His Altar was His cross.

He died that we might live. Paul was conveying this message
of Christ's death for us to the Romans when he wrote:

> "For when we were yet without strength,
> in due time Christ died for the ungodly.
> For scarcely for a righteous man will one die:
> yet peradventure for a good man some would
> even dare to die. But God commendeth his love
> toward us, in that, while we were yet sinners,
> Christ died for us" (Romans 5:6-8).

So when we today enter through the Gate and approach the
Brazen Altar, we offer ourselves – living sacrifices – holy and
acceptable to Him. We bring our sin and beg His forgiveness. We
lay on Him our iniquities, and He takes them all, giving us beauty
for ashes, light for darkness, peace for turmoil. When we repent of
our sin before Him, He makes us His righteousness. "For he hath
made him to be sin for us, who knew no sin; that we might be
made the righteousness of God in him" (II Corinthians 5:21).

CHAPTER SIX

THE LAVER OF WATER
The Place of Washing

"And the Lord spake unto Moses, saying,
Thou shalt also make a laver of brass,
and his foot also of brass, to wash withal:
and thou shalt put it between the tabernacle of the congregation
and the Altar, and thou shalt put water therein.
For Aaron and his sons shall wash their hands and their feet thereat:
When they go into the tabernacle of the congregation,
they shall wash with water, that they die not;
or when they come near to the Altar to minister,
to burn offering made by fire unto the Lord:
So they shall wash their hands and their feet, that they die not:
and it shall be a statute for ever to them,
even to him and to his seed throughout their generations."
Exodus 30:17-21

"And he made the laver of brass, and the foot of it of brass,
of the looking glasses of the women assembling,
which assembled at the door of the tabernacle of the congregation."
Exodus 38:8

THE LAVER OF WATER
The Place of Washing

The Laver of Water was a basin or large bowl filled with water placed halfway between the Brazen Altar and the Holy Place. It is interesting that in all the specifications given by God for virtually every other area, there were no specific dimensions for the Laver except that it was to be made entirely of bronze. While other pieces of furniture were wood overlaid with bronze or brass, this one piece was entirely cast of bronze.

It obviously needed to be large enough for the priests to wash both their hands and their feet in it before they entered The Holy Place and when they exited. The scripture speaks of it having at least two parts – referring to the "laver of brass" and "the foot of it." It is possible the bowl of it was placed on a foot or pedestal, so it was at least slightly elevated rather than placed at ground level. In all probability, the "pedestal" or foot was designed to itself contain water for the priests to wash their feet and legs, while the upper "bowl" was for washing their hands, arms, and upper body. Some scholars believe that it could possibly have even been large enough for the priests to sit or lie down in to wash themselves of the residue from the sacrifices.

One detail about the Laver of Water that was explicitly clear was its placement. It was to be strategically placed between the

Altar and the tabernacle. The priests were the ones who took the steps from the Altar into the tabernacle. Standing at the Altar, no doubt both their hands and feet were spattered by the their participation in offering blood sacrifices. Wind blowing against the sand and dirt of the desert floor of the Outer Court would not remove the stains from their feet or from their hands. Cleansing was needed before any further work could be done.

Made of mirrors, and filled with clean water, the Laver of Water was the place where they not only washed their hands and feet, but where they caught a glimpse of their own faces. In this mirrored bowl, they saw both their reflection in the water and in the bowl itself. They could see who they were and who they were becoming.

The washing was both literal and spiritual. It was a reminder to all people that cleansing was required before approaching God. As sinful man approaches his holy God, atonement is not enough. Cleansing is required. Once sins were atoned for at the Brazen Altar, there was the necessity of cleansing before the priests were allowed to serve in The Holy Place.

A Note About The Priestly Garments

As with other details of the Tabernacle in the Wilderness, God gave specific instructions even about the garments to be worn by the priests when in service in the Holy Place and Holy of Holies.

Aaron, the brother of Moses, was designated to be the first high priest to serve, with his sons, in the Wilderness Tabernacle – and with that designation came the basic instructions for their garments in Exodus 28:1-4:

"And take thou unto thee Aaron thy brother, and
his sons with him, from among the children of
Israel, that he may minister unto me in the priest's
office, even Aaron, Nadab and Abihu, Eleazar and
Ithamar, Aaron's sons. And thou shalt make holy
garments for Aaron thy brother for glory and for
beauty. And thou shalt speak unto all that are wise
hearted, whom I have filled with the spirit of
wisdom, that they may make Aaron's garments to
consecrate him, that he may minister unto me in
the priest's office.And these are the garments which
they shall make; a breastplate, and an ephod, and a
robe, and a broidered coat, mitre, and a girdle: and
they shall make holy garments for Aaron thy
brother, and his sons, that he may minister unto me
in the priest's office."

In Exodus 25, when God gave Moses the instructions on what
to collect in offering from the children of Israel, He specifically
requested in verse 7: "onyx stones, and stones to be set in the
ephod, and in the breastplate." These were for the priestly
garments that were to be created for Aaron and his sons to wear in
their service in the tabernacle. These beautiful and costly stones
were to be set in a specific design as noted in Exodus 28:9-12:

"And thou shalt take two onyx stones, and grave
on them the names of the children of Israel:
Six of their names on one stone, and the other
six names of the rest on the other stone, according
to their birth. With the work of an engraver in
stone, like the engravings of a signet, shalt thou
engrave the two stones with the names of the
children of Israel: thou shalt make them to be
set in ouches of gold. And thou shalt put the
two stones upon the shoulders of the ephod for
stones of memorial unto the children of Israel:

and Aaron shall bear their names before the Lord
upon his two shoulders for a memorial."

We are told in Leviticus, the priests changed clothes before
removing the ashes from the Brazen Altar to outside the camp
(Leviticus 6:3-4). We know the priests also changed from one
robe into another when moving from the Outer Court into the
Holy Place. There was still another garment worn by the High
Priest when he entered the Holy of Holies.

Having worn their regular robes for their duties offering
sacrifices at the Brazen Altar, the priests moved across the
courtyard to the Laver of Water. After washing themselves clean of
the residue from the sacrifices made for their own sins as well as
the sins of others, the priests changed robes. This robe to be worn
when entering the Holy Place is described in Exodus 28:31-35:

> "And thou shalt make the robe of the ephod
> all of blue. And there shall be an hole in the top
> of it, in the midst thereof: it shall have a binding
> of woven work round about the hole of it, as it
> were the hole of an habergeon, that it be not rent.
> And beneath upon the hem of it thou shalt make
> pomegranates of blue, and of purple, and of scarlet,
> round about the hem thereof; and bells of gold
> between them round about: A golden bell and a
> pomegranate, a golden bell and a pomegranate,
> upon the hem of the robe round about. And it
> shall be upon Aaron to minister: and his sound
> shall be heard when he goeth in unto the holy
> place before the Lord, and when he cometh out,
> that he die not."

THE PURPOSE, POWER, AND PATTERN

The Purpose of the Laver of Water was obviously to provide a place of washing for the priests who had been sullied by handling the sacrifices of the people. They could not bring their own sin, nor the residuals of the sins of the people, into the Holy Place. Therefore, washing with water was needed.

Placed between the Brazen Altar (the place of our repentance) and the Holy Place (the place of His presence) was the Laver of Water. This is the place in our prayer when we take time to read the Word of God and allow it to wash us clean. It is a time of deliberate meditation on the Word. It is the intentional washing of the Word for sanctification and cleansing.

We have entered the Gate with offerings of thanksgiving and praise. We have magnified and glorified His name. We have prayed prayers of repentance. We have humbly offered ourselves a living sacrifice to Jesus Christ and His purpose and work in us. Now we find ourselves at the Laver of Water.

While in the types and shadows of Old Testament and New, this is the place symbolic of the burial of Jesus Christ and water baptism in His name; it is also the place of sanctification. We pause in our prayer time to allow the work of the Word in us. This was a place of physical washing; the priests were instructed to wash their hands and feet before performing any ministry beyond that point. This washing – cleansing – is preparation for prayer not only for yourself but for others.

The Power of washing for the priests of that day and time was significant. However, its significance for us today is immeasurable. In John 15:3, Jesus said, "Now ye are clean through the word which I have spoken unto you." Just as we all need to practice daily personal hygiene – bathing, brushing our teeth, taking care of hair – how much more should we be attentive to daily cleansing our lives before Him? That cleansing comes by the Word of God read and spoken aloud, as prayer and promises claimed.

Ephesians speaks of the sanctification and cleansing that comes "with the washing of water by the word" (Ephesians 5:26). In the same way the sacrificed animals of old had to be without spot or blemish, we find similar terminology in this passage in Ephesians when the Bride of Christ is described as "a glorious church, not having spot, or wrinkle, or any such thing; but that it should be holy and without blemish" (Ephesians 5:27).

In Romans 8:5 we read, "For they that are after the flesh do mind the things of the flesh; but they that are after the Spirit the things of the Spirit." We must be washed clean from our sinful nature. The residual effects of what we repented of at the Brazen Altar must be washed away at the Laver of Water. By washing ourselves in the Word of God, we are able to strip off our sinful nature and take on the nature of Christ our Lord.

I Peter 2:1-5 tells us:

> "Wherefore laying aside all malice, and all guile,
> and hypocrisies, and envies, and all evil speakings,
> As newborn babes, desire the sincere milk of the
> word, that ye may grow thereby: If so be ye have
> tasted that the Lord is gracious. To whom coming,
> as unto a living stone, disallowed indeed of men, but
> chosen of God, and precious, Ye also, as lively stones,
> are built up a spiritual house, an holy priesthood,
> to offer up spiritual sacrifices, acceptable to God
> by Jesus Christ."

At the Laver of Water, we find the "sincere milk of the Word" that brings us spiritual growth. We wash ourselves with His Word, cleansing our hands and feet from the debris of our day's activities. There are sixty-six books in the Bible. It is here we let the work of all of these books be accomplished in our individual lives. From Genesis to Revelation, the power of the Word becomes ours.

The Pattern of the work of sanctification that comes at this Laver of Water, is a work of the Holy Ghost in you as a New Testament born-again believer. The cleansing that occurs here prepares you for the next level of consecration. We find here the final judgment on our spiritual cleanness.

The Laver was made of bronze – a substance symbolic in the Old Testament of the judgment of God. This laver, with its water for cleansing and its mirror for reflection, was the final place where there was full and complete cleansing for the priests. For us, it is at this Laver we examine ourselves and check our reflection in the Word and let the Word bring complete and total cleansing to us.

Could the reason no specific dimensions are given for this piece of furniture be that God wanted us to understand there is no limit to what He can do? Regardless of the depth of the stains of your sin, He can wash them all away. Nothing in your past is so vile or so powerful it cannot be erased by His blood. There is nothing in your present He cannot wash away.

The Psalmist wrote, "As far as the east is from the west, *so* far hath he removed our transgressions from us" (Psalm 103:12). Isaiah quoted, "I, even I, am he that blotteth out thy transgressions for mine own sake, and will not remember thy sins" (Isaiah 43:25). There is nothing as powerful against sin as His blood!

As the lyric of the old hymn penned by Anna Waterman in the 1920s testifies to us:

> Come, ye sinners, lost and hopeless,
> Jesus' blood can make you free;
> For He saved the worst among you,
> When He saved a wretch like me
> And I know, yes, I know
> Jesus' blood can make the vilest sinner clean,
> (www. http://library.timelesstruths.org/music/Yes_I_Know/)

You cannot have a successful, effective prayer life without the Word of God. What it is and what it promises are integral to our spiritual life and especially our individual prayer lives. In this Tabernacle of Moses, before the priests could move any closer to the presence of the Lord they had to take the time to wash at the Laver of Water. It was not a step to be done hurriedly. They had to wash both their hands and their feet. They had to make certain there were no remnants of what had gone on before that moment lingering on them. Before they could move from the Outer Court through the entrance of the tabernacle, there had to be a cleansing of their bodies and thereby their spirits.

Today, the scripture becomes our reflecting basin of cleansing water. As we read and study and pray the Word, it comes alive and brings us cleansing. It is here we follow the instruction of Peter and wash away "all malice, and all guile, and hypocrisies, and envies, and all evil speakings…" (I Peter 2:1). It is here we lay claim to being men and women with clean hands and pure hearts before God Almighty, having been washed by His blood and His Word.

CHAPTER SEVEN

THE FIVE PILLARS
Strong Enough to Lean On

"And thou shalt make an hanging for the door of the tent, of blue, and purple, and scarlet, and fine twined linen wrought with needlework. And thou shalt make for the hanging five pillars of shittim wood, and overlay them with gold, and their books shall be of gold: and thou shalt cast five sockets of brass for them."
Exodus 26:36-37

chapter seven

THE FIVE PILLARS
Strong Enough to Lean On

God did not dictate to Moses just the definition of the Outer Court and the pieces of furniture there. The attention to detail continued in the directions for the tabernacle, the Holy Place and Holy of Holies itself. As mentioned before, the dimensions of the Outer Court were specific: 100 cubits x 50 cubits. The dimensions given for the tabernacle were equally specific. It was to be 30 cubits x 10 cubits.

The thirty-cubit length was to be divided at the twenty-cubit line, creating two rooms. The first, the Holy Place, was 10 cubits x 20 cubits. The remaining room, the Holy of Holies, was 10 cubits x 10 cubits.

In the language and measurements of today, the Tabernacle of Moses was itself 44.291 feet x 14.764 feet. This then, when furnished with the instruments of the tabernacle designated for that space, including the five pillars and the draperies that divided the Holy Place from the Holy of Holies, created the 10 cubit x 20 cubit room that is called the Holy of Holies.

The common people approached the tabernacle through the designated Entrance Gate. They were given entrance into the

Outer Court, where their sacrifices were offered on the Brazen Altar. From there, the Laver of Water and the tabernacle itself were designated for the priests only. Once the priest had washed at the Laver of Water, he could enter the Holy Place through the curtains hung between the Five Pillars. In that room, the priest would see the Table of Shewbread to his right, the Golden Candlestick to the left, and the Altar of Incense in front of him. Just behind that Altar hung the Veil that separated the Holy Place from the Holy of Holies. The Outer Court objects were all made of bronze. Inside the tent, these tabernacle furnishings were made of gold.

Fire from the Brazen Altar was brought to the Altar of Incense. It was clearly stated that the fire was to never go out. Leviticus 6:13 shares the instruction, "The fire shall ever be burning upon the Altar; it shall never go out." The oil in the candlestick was ever-burning. Exodus 27:20 explains part of the process: "And thou shalt command the children of Israel, that they bring thee pure oil olive beaten for the light, to cause the lamp to burn always."

It was inside the Holy Place where the priests represented the people of Israel before Jehovah God. Representing the twelve tribes of Israel, they placed twelve loaves of unleavened bread on the Table of Shewbread. (This bread was eaten by the priests inside the Holy Place and removed every Sabbath to be replaced with fresh loaves of bread.) The priests were also responsible for the menorah – the Golden Candlestick that was the only source of light in the Holy Place. The third element in the Holy Place – the Altar of Incense – was where the priests were responsible for burning sweet smelling incense before the Lord every morning and every evening. There was a morning and an evening sacrifice every day. In addition, it was from this Altar, during the annual rite of the High Priest entering the Holy of Holies, that coals and incense from the Altar were transported beyond the Veil to the Ark of the Covenant.

As you step from the Outer Court through the Five Pillars into the Holy Place, you step inside a tented, protected area away from the elements of desert wind, rain, heat, and cold. You see the dancing candlelight and the reflections of the beautiful tapestries. Yet, you are standing on dirt – simple desert sand. It stands to reason that since it was a place where the priests traveled every day that their pathways would eventually be packed down, perhaps more than the rest. However, in the midst of the breathtaking beauty of the tapestries and candlelight, gold and silver fixtures, the sand was perhaps a reminder that this place – this Holy Place – is a place where God, the all-powerful and holy Creator, meets with His creation...man formed first out of the dust of the earth. "Then the Lord God formed a man from the dust of the ground and breathed into his nostrils the breath of life, and the man became a living being" (Genesis 2:7).

THE PURPOSE, POWER, AND PATTERN

The Purpose of the Five Pillars in the plan given to Moses for the construction of the tabernacle was much more than just to provide curtained walls of definition and an entryway into the Holy Place. While the furniture in the Outer Court dealt with the problem of sin, providing a place for repentance and sacrifice and a place for washing, cleansing, and sanctification, the Holy Place was a place of worship and communion. Until sin is dealt with in our lives, we cannot expect to find a place of communion with a high and holy God. Sin must be settled at the cross before there can be real worship.

There was a door that led from the Outer Court into the Holy Place. The priest, having offered the prayer offering, must now pass through the door of the tabernacle to come to a place of worship. Jesus Christ proclaimed, "I am the door…" in John 10:7 and 10:9. So must we, in praying through our own Tabernacle Prayer Plan, pass through the Entrance Gate. We must offer our repentance and ourselves as sacrifice to the most high God. Our last stop in that Outer Court is at the Laver of Water where we finally deal with the last remnants of our sin and are washed clean before we can enter into the Holy Place.

We then approach the door that will allow us access to the Holy Place. The door was attached by gold hooks to the Five Pillars that were made of acacia wood. They were both overlaid and capped with gold and fixed in sockets of brass. This door, leading from the Outer Court into the Holy Place, separated the place of sacrifice from the place of worship. The priest, having made the prayer offering, must now pass through the door of the tabernacle to enter the place of worship.

The Power of this aspect of tabernacle prayer is that it helps us ever step nearer to the presence of God in us. In the Old Testament, the repentant ones could only enter the courtyard and walk forward to the Altar. That was as close as the priest could get to the physical presence of God manifested in the pillar of cloud and fire inside the Holy of Holies. The rest of the rites and rituals had to be completed by the priest. However, for us today, God has given us, as His children, access to His presence. We can, like the priests, now wash and walk into the Holy Place and press into the

Holy of Holies where we begin to know and experience His glory and power.

The Pattern to incorporate this unique five pillar aspect of prayer in your daily pursuit of the presence of God is integral. This unique link to Isaiah's description of the Messiah can be easily applied to the needs that are present in each of our lives and the lives of those with whom we do life. From casual acquaintances to our closest friends and family members, the power of praying for those in our lives to know the wonder of His presence becomes a wonderful prayer of progression. We pray for them to gain His wise and wonderful counsel in any area of concern in their lives, to know that He is mighty to save and deliver them, to discover Him as their Father, and to know Him as their Prince of Peace.

In my father's prayer time, he linked the Five Pillars to the five roles of Jesus Christ identified in Isaiah's prophecy in Isaiah 9:6:

> "For unto us a child is born, unto us a son is given:
> and the government shall be upon his shoulder:
> and his name shall be called wonderful, counselor,
> the mighty God, the everlasting father,
> and the prince of peace."

This was where Dad did his most fervent intercessory prayer. It was as if he imagined these five pillars attached to the door of the tabernacle, and he would pray diligently for the needs of others. He would pray for specific people and specific needs – from the members of our family to missionaries on foreign fields. He prayed for Israel and world leadership.

He prayed in the name of Jesus, who said, "...And whatsoever ye shall ask in my name, that will I do..." (John 14:13).

With each of the Five Pillars, he prayed for different groups of people and different needs. Often he called people by name as the Lord would quicken them to his remembrance. Other times, he would pray more generally.

Wonderful – He prayed for his family.
> He called each of us by name and prayed
> for whatever came to mind for us.

Counselor – He prayed for our church families and leadership.
> He prayed for the wisdom of God for those
> in business and involved in Kingdom enterprise.

The Mighty God – Here my dad would brag on God.
> He prayed to Him as the almighty and all powerful
> God of the universe. It is here he would pray God's
> intervention in situations that required the action
> of a mighty God.

The Everlasting Father – He prayed for those in need of "fatherly" attention.
> He prayed for those with sickness and disease.
> He prayed for the incarcerated and institutionalized.
> He prayed by name for the widows and orphans and
> those feeling abandoned and alone in the world.

The Prince of Peace – He prayed for peace.
> At this time my father prayed for peace in our lives,
> our homes, our schools, and our churches. He prayed
> for peace in the world political arena. Without fail,
> he prayed for the peace of Jerusalem.

It was here, at this entrance to the Holy Place, that, as my Dad prayed for peace, he would go on to quote Isaiah 9:7: "Of the increase of his government and peace there shall be no end. . ."

Jesus, in John 14:27, where He gave some of His final words to His disciples, promised, "My peace I leave with you, my peace I give unto you: not as the world giveth, give I unto you. Let not your heart be troubled, neither let it be afraid." There is perhaps no greater need among us than for God-given "peace that passeth all understanding" (Philippians 4:7).

Our world today – your world – is in need of the Five Pillars of prayer. Your family needs to be covered with prayer. Wisdom is needed in relationships, both personal and professional. The power and glory of God need to go on display before a lost world. There are sinners in need of a Savior to rescue and redeem them. There are those who need to know the love and tender mercy of a loving Father. And we all need a little peace.

The world is in need of peace. Individuals need the peace of God. Families are in turmoil and strife and need the peace of God. Our country – every city and community and state - needs the peace of God. Our world needs the peace of God as never before. It is in this place that petitions for those who know Him and need to know Him can be made known unto Him who is the child born and son given and whose name shall be called "Wonderful, Counselor, the mighty God, the everlasting Father, the Prince of Peace" (Isaiah 9:6).

CHAPTER EIGHT

THE HOLY PLACE
The Place of Meeting

"And thou shalt make boards for the tabernacle of shittim wood standing up. Ten cubits shall be the length of a board, and a cubit and a half shall be the breadth of one board. Two tenons shall there be in one board, set in order one against another: thus shalt thou make for all the boards of the tabernacle. And thou shalt make the boards for the tabernacle, twenty boards on the south side southward. And thou shalt make forty sockets of silver under the twenty boards; two sockets under one board for his two tenons, and two sockets under another board for his two tenons. And for the second side of the tabernacle on the north side there shall be twenty boards: And their forty sockets of silver; two sockets under one board, and two sockets under another board. And for the sides of the tabernacle westward thou shalt make six boards. And two boards shalt thou make for the corners of the tabernacle in the two sides. And they shall be coupled together beneath, and they shall be coupled together above the head of it unto one ring: thus shall it be for them both; they shall be for the two corners.

And they shall be eight boards, and their sockets of silver, sixteen sockets; two sockets under one board, and two sockets under another board. And thou shalt make bars of shittim wood; five for the boards of the one side of the tabernacle, And five bars for the boards of the other side of the tabernacle, and five bars for the boards of the side of the tabernacle, for the two sides westward. And the middle bar in the midst of the boards shall reach from end to end. And thou shalt overlay the boards with gold, and make their rings of gold for places for the bars: and thou shalt overlay the bars with gold. And thou shalt rear up the tabernacle according to the fashion thereof which was shewed thee in the mount"

Exodus 26:15-30

chapter eight

THE HOLY PLACE
The Place of Meeting

Once again, we see the detail and precision of the instructions given to Moses and hear that overlying rule of order: "according to the fashion thereof which was shewed thee in the mount" (Exodus 26:30). There was to be a frame built for the tabernacle. On that frame would be a series of hangings to create and complete the tent. The first part of this process was to make 48 upright supports – 10 cubits x 1.5 cubits (approximately 14.75 feet x 2.417 feet).

These boards used to construct the tabernacle were not solid planks but were rather constructed into frames. The two long boards were connected – top, middle, and base – by cross rails. While, first of all, the acacia tree in Sinai generally does not grow to such a size to readily supply a 27 inch solid plank, this open construction would make the structure lighter and easier to move when necessary. In addition, the fine linen with its embroidered cherubim would be seen between the framing. In the construction process, the wood would have been cut, stripped, and dried before being overlaid with pure gold. Placed in the upright position as noted, there were twenty placed along the north and south sides, while the rear wall had only eight. Two of these eight were placed on the western corners, forming a type of buttress.

Remember, the front of the tabernacle, the entrance to the Holy Place, was supported by the Five Pillars. These were constructed of acacia wood, overlaid with gold and set in bronze bases.

Exodus 26:36-37 explains:

> "And thou shalt make an hanging for the door of
> the tent, of blue, and purple, and scarlet, and fine
> twined linen, wrought with needlework. And
> thou shalt make for the hanging five pillars of
> shittim wood, and overlay them with gold,
> and their hooks shall be of gold: and thou shalt
> cast five sockets of brass for them."

This upright frame was secured into two sockets made of silver. Each socket was specifically designed so an extension on one side arm of the frame fit into it in the form of a tenon. It was these silver sockets that formed a continuous foundation around the three sides of the framework. W. Shaw Caldecott further explains tenon here:

> "This word, occurring in Exodus 26 and 36, is used
> in the account of the tabernacle to describe the
> "hand" or yadh by which its 48 boards were kept in
> place. Each board had two tenons which were
> mortised into it (Exodus 36:22). These tenons
> would be made of harder wood than the acacia, so
> as better to stand the strain of wind and weather.
> When in use the tenons were sunk into the
> 'sockets,' and allowed for a speedy re-erection of the
> tabernacle at its every move. Sockets are also
> mentioned as in use for the standards of the
> tabernacle court (Exodus 27:10), but there is no
> mention of tenons. It may be that

the base of each standard was let into its socket, without the use of any tenon. This would give it sufficient stability, as the height of each standard was but 5 cubits (7 1/2 feet) (Exodus 27:18)" (W. Shaw Caldecott/International Standard Bible Encyclopedia at biblestudytools.com).

The system of frames, rings, and bars helped make the interior walls of the tabernacle solid. Golden rings, strategically placed top, bottom, and center of the frame, were for supporting bars (made of acacia wood) to be inserted. These bars then held the row of frames together. There were five bars on each side. There was a middle bar that ran from end to end the entire length of one side. The other two bars – for the top and bottom rings – ran halfway along each side.

There was a specific order and detailed instruction on what was to be hung inside and draped outside of this structure. Inside the Holy Place, hung where they could be seen through the framework, were to be the elaborate linen curtains. Next were to be goat skins, again with specific numbers and dimensions. Then Exodus 26:16 simply instructed them, "And thou shalt make a covering for the tent of rams' skins dyed red, and a covering above of badgers' skins." Despite the beauty of the interior, the exterior of this edifice was not appealing or comely. To the casual on-looker, there was no indication on the outside of the beauty within.

It is interesting to note that with all of this attention to detail and elaborate instructions for fine linen and wood overlain with gold, the tabernacle had no floor. There were no gold-covered boards, no specially raised platform to step up into the Holy Place. The floor was simply sand, the dirt of the desert. When the priests stepped into the Holy Place, what they saw was the reflection of gold that encased all the wood used to construct the walls. Unseen, below the ground, were the sockets of silver. Still, they were standing on the sand of the desert place in which they wandered and camped. The floor of God's dwelling place was dust – the stuff from which man was made from and to which he returns. Perhaps it was a reminder that, despite their dealings with God on high, they were also bound to earth below.

From the Entrance Gate to the multi-stages of the animal skin coverings, from the embroidered linen to the fine silver and gold, even to the dirt floor, everything was set by God, delivered to Moses, and carried out by skilled workers chosen of God. It was all to be done according to the specifications given to Moses: "And thou shalt rear up the tabernacle according to the fashion thereof which was shewed thee in the mount" (Exodus 26:30).

THE PURPOSE, POWER, AND PATTERN

We know the outside walls of this Wilderness Tabernacle were unappealing. The perimeter of the Outer Court was delineated by white linen curtains that would no doubt glisten in the wilderness sun, a thing of beauty in the midst of the desert. Once inside the court, though, you realize the exterior appearance of the tabernacle was deceptive. The layer of skins both protected and hid the beauty of the gold fixtures and beautifully embroidered linens within.

It brings to mind Isaiah's description of the Savior to come in Isaiah 53:2; "…he hath no form nor comeliness; and when we shall see him, *there is* no beauty that we should desire him."

The actual ceiling of this sanctuary for God was the curtains of fine linen. It has been mentioned before that this white linen, whether adorned with embroidery or not, was symbolic of righteousness. The next layer, goat's hair, was placed over the fine linen. This is symbolic of the sin offering. It was specified that the ram's skin was to be dyed red. This third level symbolizes substitution. Jesus took our place! He that knew no sin became sin. The final layer, from skins of badgers, was what the world outside saw first. It provided protection from the desert weather with its unrelenting heat and sudden storms.

The Purpose for us today is that when we walk through the entrance to the Holy Place, we find ourselves in a place where Jesus Christ becomes our covering. He is our righteousness. He is the Lamb that was slain from the foundation of the world. He is our substitute, once and for all. He is our protection. He covers us and protects us from the onslaught of the enemy against our souls by the power that is in His name and His blood.

The sockets of silver that supported the Holy Place and the Holy of Holies were costly, each one made with a talent of silver. God required precious metal for the foundation of this place of His dwelling. Yet, these sockets were, in all probability, buried in the dirt, not seen by human eyes. While this specific instruction is not given in the scriptural text, it is a logical assumption that anything that is standing on sand could be blown over. If the sockets were at least partially buried, it gave strength to the posts and kept the posts from blowing over. So it is in the New Testament we find Paul writing that he was, like an expert builder laying a foundation but noting that it was not a typical foundation but was, in fact, Jesus Christ and only Jesus Christ; "For other foundation can no man lay than that is laid, which is Jesus Christ" (I Corinthians 3:11).

The Power of this Holy Place was that the priests did the work of the Kingdom herein. They tended the Table of Shewbread, made sure there was oil in the Golden Candlestick, burnt incense at the Altar and offered both morning and evening sacrifices to God. It was a place where, perpetually, the priests could come near to the presence of God. Just on the other side of the Veil stood the Ark of the Covenant, dwelling place of the Most High.

The Pattern, in this room of the tabernacle, brings us to a place where we pause briefly to focus ourselves on where we have been and where we are going. We have entered through the Entrance Gate with prayers of thanksgiving and praise. We have stepped up to the Brazen Altar and placed ourselves as a sacrifice in true repentance and surrender. We have washed with the Word in preparation for serving Him. We've progressed past the Five Pillars and prayed for revelation power to be present in us and through us. And now, we are ready, in this Holy Place, to continue the journey into His shekinah presence.

CHAPTER NINE

THE GOLDEN CANDLESTICK
The Place of Anointing & Direction

*"And thou shalt make a candlestick of pure gold: of beaten work
shall the candlestick be made: his shaft, and his branches, his bowls,
his knops, and his flowers, shall be of the same. And six branches shall
come out of the sides of it; three branches of the candlestick out of the one
side, and three branches of the candlestick out of the other side:
Three bowls made like unto almonds, with a knop and a flower
in one branch; and three bowls made like almonds in the other branch,
with a knop and a flower: so in the six branches that come out of the
candlestick. And in the candlesticks shall be four bowls made like unto
almonds, with their knops and their flowers. And there shall be a knop
under two branches of the same, and a knop under two branches of the
same, and a knop under two branches of the same,
according to the six branches that proceed out of the candlestick.
Their knops and their branches shall be of the same:
all it shall be one beaten work of pure gold. And thou shalt make the
seven lamps thereof: and they shall light the lamps thereof,
that they may give light over against it. And the tongs thereof, and the
snuffdishes thereof, shall be of pure gold. Of a talent of pure gold
shall he make it, with all these vessels.
And look that thou make them after their pattern,
which was shewed thee in the mount."*
Exodus 25:31-40

chapter nine

THE GOLDEN CANDLESTICK
The Place of Anointing and Direction

The first piece of furniture we encounter in the Holy Place is the Golden Candlestick. It was a seven-stemmed candelabra. We read in Exodus 25 once again the specific instructions concerning the bowls and flowers and knobs and branches of the Golden Candlestick, along with the fact that it was to be "one beaten work of pure gold" (Exodus 25:36). This passage, this description of the Candlestick, echoed again "make them after their pattern, which was shewed thee in the mount" (Exodus 25:40).

As the priest stepped through the curtains of the entryway, his eyes would be drawn to the dancing light of the seven burning flames of the Golden Candlestick. There was no light from outside allowed inside the Holy Place. In this spiritual place, there was no room for human reasoning and the philosophies of man. This was God's dwelling place, and it was a Holy Place.

While it is referred to as a candlestick, it was, in effect, an oil lamp. Scripture mentions this holy vessel thirty times. The lamp had a central stem – the candlestick was center – with three branches on each side. Once again, like with the Laver of Water outside this tabernacle, we find there were no dimensions given. Perhaps, again, this omission is indicative of the limitlessness of the light of God. It was constructed from a solid piece of gold beaten into shape, weighing close to 100 pounds. Its monetary value today may be well over $30,000 (www.plymothbrethern.org). Today, it is known as the menorah of is, perhaps, one of the most commonly-used symbols of Judaism.

The Holy Place menorah – the Golden Candlestick – consisted of three main parts. It had a base, then the shaft or candlestick, and then the branches on either side. From the base, there was a vertical stem and then from it on, either side, there were three branches that curved outward and upward. All six branches, as well as the center stem, ended with a cup shaped like an open almond flower. At the top of the candlestick, the open petals of the flower held an oil lamp. Both the branches and the stem held the same open blossom design, three on each branch and four on the center shaft. The seven oil lamps rested in the petals like small bowls. A flax or linen wick would be placed in the lamp. This intricate design commanded by God required that only the most highly skilled of the craftsmen would even attempt to create it.

The Law commanded in Leviticus 24:2 that the fire was to never go out: "command the children of Israel, that they bring unto thee pure oil olive beaten for the light, to cause the lamps to burn continually." Consequently, twice every day the high priest trimmed and tended the wick and made sure the pure olive oil was in good supply. Leviticus 24:3 tells us it was a task assigned only to Aaron: "Without the vail of the testimony, in the tabernacle of the congregation, shall Aaron order it from the evening unto the morning before the LORD continually: *it shall be* a statute for ever in your generations."

One writer observed,

> "All day and all night, whether anyone was present
> or not, these seven lamps constantly lit up the glory
> of the Holy Place especially on the table of the
> showbread as a reminder that God's presence is
> always with His people" (bible-history.com).

While the children of Israel could always see the pillar of fire
by night and pillar of cloud by day hovering over the Holy of
Holies, light from this Golden Candlestick also was ever-present.

THE PURPOSE, POWER, AND PLAN

The Purpose of the Golden Candlestick, strategically placed in
The Holy Place, was to bring light into what would have otherwise
been a dark and foreboding room. It is in that light, too, that we
find life. Jesus said, "I am the light of the world; he that followeth
me shall not walk in darkness, but shall have the light of life" (John
8:12).

The single source of light in the Holy Place was the Golden
Candlestick. It was to shine especially on the Table of Shewbread.
It was to serve as a constant and consistent reminder to God's
children that He was there in that place dwelling with them.

The Power of the Golden Candlestick comes through the
power of light and life. John wrote of Jesus, "In him was life; and
the life was the light of men. And the light shineth in darkness;
and the darkness comprehended it not" (John 1:4-5). The light
that was Jesus Christ dispelled the darkness of sin that had
encompassed the world. He brought light and life to fallen man.
The only way man can know God is to know Jesus Christ.
Worship does not exist in darkness; it is only in the light that is

Jesus Christ Himself that true worship can come forth from the created to the Creator.

As we look at the instructions given and look for the meaning and significance of various aspects of this Golden Candlestick there are several points of spiritual application. Gold represents deity. The gold was beaten. Buds and flowers are symbolic of resurrection. Herein we see Jesus Christ. He endured the cross. He was indeed "wounded for our transgressions and bruised for our iniquities" (Isaiah 53:5). The incarnate Word, our Lord Jesus Christ, will accept no limitations. He is light and life – omnipotent, omnipresent, and omniscient. He knows no boundaries.

In John 15:5, Jesus said, "I am the vine, ye are the branches." Wrapped up in the construction of this Candlestick is a picture of our relationship with Christ. There were three branches on either side of a central stem. When Jesus said, "Ye are the light of the world" (Matthew 5:14), He was calling each of us to be light in our world to let our light "so shine before men" (Matthew 5:16). In Revelation, the gospel light shone forth from lampstands. It was all typed and shadowed in this Wilderness Tabernacle.

The Pattern for this intriguing piece of furniture is to assure that we give daily attention to keeping His light in our personal prayer lives. This is the only way possible that we might be "the light of the world" (Matthew 5:14). One writer observed, "There is no light in the world today except as the Holy Spirit sets on fire the children of God" (Snaddon, Daniel C. March 28, 2009. http://www.plymouthbrethren.org/article/11847).

Seven is a number of divine perfection. The seven lamps in this candlestick represent the light of the Holy Spirit in us. The oil represents the Holy Spirit. When the Holy Spirit begins to supernaturally work on the heart of a man or woman, it brings light – and it is a light that, if tended to properly, will never go out.

As we walk in the Spirit, we must take the time every day to give attention to the care and keeping of our light. Trimming away what used to be makes way for fresh fire and anointing. We want to see the purity of His fire, not the smoke created by stale oil and untrimmed wicks.

In the parable of the ten virgins, five wise and five foolish, found in Matthew 25, the underlying story is of ultimate importance to you and me today. It is both call and caution to keep the oil of His presence and anointing fresh and full in us. We must always allow His light to shine forth through us into this sin-darkened world. It is imperative that we not run out of oil, that we strive every day to make sure there is oil in the lantern. We must keep the wicks trimmed and the fire burning.

As has been mentioned, this Candlestick was constructed with an open flow from one tip to the next. When you poured the oil into one opening, it filled itself and the one next to it and the one next to it until all seven were filled. We must have a free flow of the oil of His Spirit in our lives in order to bring light and life to those around us. The light from the Golden Candlestick brought light and focus to the Table of Shewbread and to the Altar of Incense. Our hearts and lives, full of the oil of His Spirit, will enhance both our personal offerings of incense and our sharing of the Word with anointing and power.

CHAPTER
TEN

THE TABLE OF SHEWBREAD
The Place of Fellowship and Petition

*"Thou shalt also make a table of shittim wood:
two cubits shall be the length thereof, and a cubit the breadth thereof,
and a cubit and a half the height thereof. And thou shalt overlay it with
pure gold, and make thereto a crown of gold round about. And thou
shalt make unto it a border of an hand breadth round about, and thou
shalt make a golden crown to the border thereof round about. And thou
shalt make for it four rings of gold, and put the rings in the four corners
that are on the four feet thereof. Over against the border shall the rings
be for places of the staves to bear the table. And thou shalt make the
staves of shittim wood, and overlay them with gold, that the table may
be borne with them. And thou shalt make the dishes thereof, and spoons
thereof, and covers thereof, and bowls thereof, to cover withal: of pure
gold shalt thou make them.
And thou shalt set upon the table shewbread before me alway."*
Exodus 25:23-30

chapter ten

THE TABLE OF SHEWBREAD
The Place of Fellowship and Petition

Upon entrance into the Holy Place, the shimmering light of the room is the Golden Candlestick set to the left of the entrance. Across from it on the right is the Table of Shewbread. As has been the case with most of the furniture pieces, the Table is no exception with regard to the plan being given to Moses for specific design and size. It was to be built of acacia wood then overlaid with pure gold. It was to be rectangular in shape and to measure 2cubits x 1 cubit. It was to be 1.5 cubits tall. (35.433 inches long and 17.71 inches wide, at a height of 26.57 inches.)

There were further instructions about it having a border and a crown. There were to be four rings on the four feet and a place for the staves that bore the table to be stored. The Table was to be set with dishes and spoons and bowls and covers. Most important of all, though, was the bread. "And thou shalt set upon the table shewbread before me always" (Exodus 25:30).

There was a place to stand but no place to sit in the Holy Place. While the priests were in the Holy Place they were to be respectful of their duties and the One to whom they were offering service.

They stood to trim the wicks and pour the oil in caring for the Golden Candlestick. They stood in honor and respect for the bread that was given.

Shewbread was the term used for unleavened bread or what, in current day terms, is similar to matzoh. The Hebrew term was "sho'-bred lechem ha-panim" which means "bread of the presence." From the International Standard Bible Encyclopedia we learn the following:

> "All that the Mosaic legislation required was that, once in every week, there should be twelve cakes of unleavened bread, each containing about four-fifths of a peck of fine flour, placed in two piles upon a pure table with frankincense beside each pile and changed every Sabbath day (Leviticus 24:5-9). From the description of the table upon which the flat cakes were to lie (Exodus 25:23-30; 37:10-16), it held a series of golden vessels comprising dishes, spoons, flagons and bowls. As it is unlikely that empty cups were set before Yahweh--they being described as 'the vessels which were upon the table'— we may conclude that the table held presentation offerings of 'grain and wine and oil,' the three chief products of the land (Deuteronomy 7:13). The 'dishes' were probably the salvers on which the thin cakes were piled, six on each. The 'flagons' would contain wine, and the bowls (made with spouts, 'to pour withal'), the oil; while the 'spoons' held the frankincense, which was burned as a memorial, 'even an offering made by fire unto Yahweh.' The cakes themselves were eaten by the priests on every Sabbath day, as being among the 'most holy' sacrifices.

The Table of Shewbread – the bread of His presence – was and is a constant reminder of God's everlasting covenant with His people. The twelve loaves of bread, were significant in that He would provide for the twelve tribes of Israel. It was to be "before me alway" – at no point in the changing out of the loaves of bread was there to be even the shortest of intervals when there was no bread in the room. As the loaves were lifted off the table on the Sabbath, new loaves were in place. God desired then, and desires now, a special and uniquely uninterrupted time with His children. Bible_History.com tells us that there is a Jewish tradition, though not documented in Scripture, that there were eight priests who "passed the bread" to facilitate this transition.

Leviticus gives us the precise instructions received as a part of the Law regarding the shewbread. Leviticus 24:5-9 reads:

> "And thou shalt take fine flour, and bake twelve
> cakes thereof: two tenth deals shall be in one cake.
> And thou shalt set them in two rows, six on a
> row, upon the pure table before the Lord. And
> thou shalt put pure frankincense upon each row,
> that it may be on the bread for a memorial,
> even an offering made by fire unto the Lord.
> Every sabbath he shall set it in order before
> the Lord continually, being taken from the
> children of Israel by an everlasting covenant.
> And it shall be Aaron's and his sons'; and they
> shall eat it in the Holy Place: for it is most holy
> unto him of the offerings of the Lord made
> by fire by a perpetual statute."

The significance of the instructions for the bread is easily identifiable. It was to be fine flour – that is, taken from the earth.

It is to be baked - symbolic of suffering and agony. There is to be no leaven added; nothing artificial has a place there.

Easton's Bible Dictionary shares this insight into the meaning of the pure frankincense with which the bread was to be sprinkled:

> "An odorous resin imported from Arabia (Isaiah 60:6;
> Jeremiah 6:20), yet also growing in Palestine. It was one of
> the ingredients in the perfume of the sanctuary (Exodus
> 30:34), and was used as an accompaniment of the meat-
> offering (Leviticus 2:1 Leviticus 2:16 ; 6:15 ; 24:7). When
> burnt it emitted a fragrant odour, and hence the incense
> became a symbol of the Divine name (Malachi 1:11)
> and an emblem of prayer (Psalms 141:2 ; Luke
> 1:10; Revelation 5:8; 8:3)."

The bread was to be placed strategically on a table in two stacks of six with the frankincense on each stack. The table, in its construction, included a lip around the edge and rings for staves to be placed through them to facilitate moving this piece of furniture. In reading Numbers 4:7-8 it appears that when they did travel, the bread was not removed from the table, but rather covered and carefully transported with the dishes, etc. that were a part of this display: "And upon the table of shewbread they shall spread a cloth of blue, and put thereon the dishes, and the spoons, and the bowls, and covers to cover withal: and the continual bread shall be thereon..."

THE PURPOSE, POWER, AND PATTERN

John 6 contains two verses in which Jesus referred to Himself as bread:

> "And Jesus said unto them, I am the bread of life:
> he that cometh to me shall never hunger; and he

that believeth on me shall never thirst" (John 6:35).

"I am the living bread which came down from heaven: if any man eat of this bread, he shall live for ever: and the bread that I will give is my flesh, which I will give for the life of the world" (John 6:51)

The Purpose of the Table of Shewbread, the place where "the bread of His presence" was kept, is a reminder to us all of God's willingness to accommodate man's desire to be in His presence.

This part of Israel's worship pointed to the death of Jesus Christ on the cross. The table and its bread and wine was a type of what had been – the Passover meal. It also was a type of what was to come – Jesus' last meal with His disciples. It is a celebration of the victory Jesus Christ won over death, hell, and the grave when He gave Himself the sacrifice for all.

The Power of time spent in prayer in this place where the bread of heaven is made available to all of us produces unlimited results when we pray, for those who preach and teach the Word, sharing His bread and His presence around the world.

The arrangement of the twelve loaves always being in place is significant to us today. We always have access to the bread of His presence. He will never not be there. Whenever we call, He hears and answers.

The Pattern of time spent in prayer in this place of bread and light and life will bring strength and sustenance to us as we pray. Jesus is the bread of life. He sustains us. He keeps us, and we must keep Him, never allowing the light to go out or the bread of life to disappear from the table of our prayer.

In this time of specific prayer, my father concentrated more on the table than on the bread. It was at this juncture, he prayed for those who "hold" the bread – for missionaries, pastors, evangelists, teachers, and other leaders.

Please do not misunderstand this at this point. The bread is important. The communion between God and the priests is integral to the process. However, it was at this point that my father felt to pray that the unique needs of his fellow men and women in ministry might be met by a benevolent Heavenly Father.

This is a place where we pray for others who are called and charged with the responsibility of sharing the bread of life. It is here we pray for fresh revelation and for great spiritual awakening to come as a result of the Word at work in the lives of men and women internationally. This is where we pray, too, for ourselves to be directed to individuals in our own world who are in need of the Word.

CHAPTER ELEVEN

THE ALTAR OF INCENSE
The Place of Intercession

"And thou shalt make an Altar to burn incense upon:
of shittim wood shalt thou make it. A cubit shall be the length thereof,
and a cubit the breadth thereof; foursquare shall it be: and
two cubits shall be the height thereof: the horns thereof shall be of the
same. And thou shalt overlay it with pure gold, the top thereof, and
the sides thereof round about, and the horns thereof; and thou
shalt make unto it a crown of gold round about. And two
golden rings shalt thou make to it under the crown of it, by
the two corners thereof, upon the two sides of it shalt thou make it; and
they shall be for places for the staves to bear it withal. And thou
shalt make the staves of shittim wood, and overlay them with gold.

"And Aaron shall burn thereon sweet incense every morning: when he
dresseth the lamps, he shall burn incense upon it. And when Aaron
lighteth the lamps at even, he shall burn incense upon it, a perpetual
incense before the Lord throughout your generations. Ye shall offer no
strange incense thereon, nor burnt sacrifice, nor meat offering; neither
shall ye pour drink offering thereon. And Aaron shall make an
atonement upon the horns of it once in a year with the blood of the sin
offering of atonements: once in the year shall he make atonement upon it
throughout your generations: it is most holy unto the Lord."

Exodus 30:1-5 and 7-10

THE ALTAR OF INCENSE
The Place of Intercession

Size and design, detail-by-detail, measurement-by-measurement – it was all given to Moses. The Altar of Incense, the third piece of furniture in the Holy Place, was given as much attention as any other piece. We read in Exodus of how the Altar was to be built, and then we read exactly how it was to be used.

This Altar was to be different from the first one. It is significantly smaller than the Brazen Altar. This Altar of Incense was to be just 1 cubit^2 and 2 cubits tall. (17.71 inches square and 35.433 inches tall). It was made of acacia wood and overlaid with gold. It stood taller than both the Golden Candlestick and the Table of Shewbread. It was located straight in front of the entrance, but closest to the veil that separated the Holy Place from the Holy of Holies. Like the Brazen Altar in the Outer Court, this Altar also had four horns, these golden. It also had golden rings designed for poles to be inserted through them in order to carry the Altar when it was time to move.

This Altar was designed and used for burning incense twice a day by the priest. There were three rare spices blended with frankincense then beaten to fine powder. Salt was added. The

Law strictly forbade that this recipe be used by any private individual. Instead, it was only to be used in the worship of God in the Holy Place.

The Golden Altar was used for burning incense, which twice every day was offered by the priest after he had tended the wick and oil on the Golden Candlestick. The horns of the Altar were also sprinkled with the blood of the sin offering.

Hot coals from the Brazen Altar were brought to the Altar of Incense. It was on these hot coals the incense was burned. When the incense was poured out, the heat from the coals produced a circulating aroma in the Holy Place.

It was here the sacrifice of praise from a person whose sins were forgiven in accordance with the Law and by blood, was able to express love and worship. As the smoke and scent of the incense rose as a beautiful fragrance before God, so did the worship from His children.

The formula was given to Moses for creating the incense that was to be burned on this Altar. As noted, this was totally forbidden for this formula to be used by any private individual and for any other purpose than as an offering to Jehovah God. It had to be used only in the worship of God in the Holy Place.

The recipe for this incense was very specific. Added, in equal parts, to a set amount of frankincense, were stacte, onycha, and galbanum (Exodus 30:34). Stacte is a powder created from crushing to powder the hardened drops of the fragrant bark of a myrrh bush. Onycha is the powder from a Red Sea mollusk. Galbanum has a musky pungent smell and is considered valuable because it has the capability of preserving the scent of mixed perfumes and fragrances. It allows distribution of the scent over a long period of time. This particular combination – in these ratios – was the only acceptable incense for the Holy Place.

It is here we again see Jesus, this time a part of the sweetness of prayer. Ephesians 5:2 says, "And walk in love, as Christ also has loved us and given Himself for us, an offering and a sacrifice to God for a sweet smelling aroma." We offer ourselves to Him; we offer the sacrifice of our praise and worship to Him. He accepts our sacrifice and responds to our worship and praise.

THE PURPOSE, POWER, AND PATTERN

Each step in this Tabernacle journey has brought us closer and closer to the Holy of Holies. This Altar, separated from the Ark of the Covenant and the Holy of Holies by nothing more than a fabric veil, speaks to us of worship. We see Him as our High Priest. He is our mediator. He is our Savior. His sacrifice at Calvary makes our worship possible today.

It is estimated a common priest would, at least seven hundred times a year, burn this fragrant incense before the Lord and offer the sacrifice of worship. He knew this place and this act brought him as close as he would ever get to the full presence of God. Only the High Priest was ever allowed to go beyond this point and, even then, only on the Day of Atonement once a year.

The Purpose of the Altar of Incense was to provide a place where incense could be offered both morning and evening. It was the place where the priest brought fire from the Brazen Altar and made certain the incense was properly offered.

It was a place of offering, a sacrifice that was, in fact, "a sweet smelling savor" to the Lord (Ephesians 5:2). It was here, as the priest mixed the incense to be offered, that once again the purity of the offering was required. Ecclesiastes 10:1 tells us, "Dead flies cause the ointment of the apothecary to send forth a stinking savour…" Everything that was used had to be to the exact specifications and requirements set by God Himself. They dare not offer a stinking "savour" to a pure and holy God.

In addition to keeping the Golden Candlestick aglow, and bread on the Table, it was also the priest's responsibility to keep the incense burning at all times. Thus, it is incumbent upon us to make sure that everything is in order and to trust that He is working for our good.

The Power of this aspect of Tabernacle Prayer is that it serves as a reminder that Jesus Christ Himself is ever interceding for us. This Golden Altar is type and shadow of Jesus Christ who is our intercessor and whose prayers for us are never ceasing. To Simon Peter Jesus said, "I have prayed for you."

One writer observed, "The incense was fueled by the fire from the Altar. It is not just anyone praying for us but the King himself…" (https://www.bible-history.com/tabernacle/TAB4The_Golden_Altar_of_Incense.htm).

Hebrews 7:22-25 tells us:

> "By so much was Jesus made a surety of a better testament. And they truly were many priests, because they were not suffered to continue by reason of death: But this man, because he continueth ever, hath an unchangeable priesthood. Wherefore he is able also to save them to the uttermost that come unto God by him, seeing he ever liveth to make intercession for them."

The Pattern. At this juncture in our prayer journey, we ponder the Altar of Incense and its details and value our time of prayer as a time of sacrifice to the Lord. The incense is symbolic of our worship. The fact that the fire that burns it never goes out is a reminder to us that Jesus Himself is interceding for us.

The apothecary formula was given – equal parts of frankincense, stacte, onycha, and galbanum. Each of the components were the product of some form of breaking and crushing to get to an oil form that could be burned at the Altar of Incense. It was also specifically forbidden for use for any other purpose than offering at the Altar of Incense. This testifies to the uniqueness of not just the piece of furniture, but to the process.

This is the place where we make every need known to a God who not only hears but answers our prayers. There is not a word of prayer from this place that goes unheard. It is a time and place of intercession for our needs and the needs of our friends and family. It is a time of intervening prayer that dispatches angels. It is this kind of prayer that changes lives for eternity.

CHAPTER TWELVE

THE HOLY OF HOLIES
THE PLACE OF HIS PRESENCE
The Veil and the Ark

"And thou shalt make a vail of blue, and purple, and scarlet, and fine twined linen of cunning work: with cherubims shall it be made: And thou shalt hang it upon four pillars of shittim wood overlaid with gold: their hooks shall be of gold, upon the four sockets of silver. And thou shalt hang up the vail under the taches, that thou mayest bring in thither within the vail the ark of the testimony: and the vail shall divide unto you between the Holy Place and the most holy."
Exodus 26:31-33

"And they shall make an ark of shittim wood: two cubits and a half shall be the length thereof, and a cubit and a half the breadth thereof, and a cubit and a half the height thereof. And thou shalt overlay it with pure gold, within and without shalt thou overlay it, and shalt make upon it a crown of gold round about. And thou shalt cast four rings of gold for it, and put them in the four corners thereof; and two rings shall be in the one side of it, and two rings in the other side of it. And thou shalt make staves of shittim wood, and overlay them with gold. And thou shalt put the staves into the rings by the sides of the ark, that the ark may be borne with them."
"And thou shalt make a Mercy Seat of pure gold: two cubits and a half shall be the length thereof, and a cubit and a half the breadth thereof. ¹⁸ *And thou shalt make two cherubims of gold, of beaten work shalt thou make them, in the two ends of the Mercy Seat. And make one cherub on the one end, and the other cherub on the other end: even of the Mercy Seat shall ye make the cherubims on the two ends thereof. And the cherubims shall stretch forth their wings on high, covering the Mercy Seat with their wings, and their faces shall look one to another; toward the Mercy Seat shall the faces of the cherubims be."*
Exodus 25:10-14 and 17-20

chapter twelve

THE HOLY OF HOLIES
The Place of His Presence,
The Veil, and the Ark

The Veil hung between the Holy Place and the Holy of Holies. It was the final separation between man and God. Though it was made of finely spun white linen with blue and purple and scarlet similar to those surrounding the Holy of Holies, this was different. It was to never be touched except once a year when the High Priest entered to sprinkle blood on the Mercy Seat on the Day of Atonement.

It is here we find the second set of four columns. We first found the columns and symbolism of the four Gospels at the Entrance Gate. Here, at the place where the multi-layered Veil separates the Holy Place from the Holy of Holies we find them again. These four columns, just like those at the Entrance Gate, represent the Gospels of Jesus Christ – Matthew, Mark, Luke, and John. Three of the four Gospels specifically mention the Veil being rent from top to bottom (Matthew 27:51, Mark 15:38, Luke 23:45). Symbolically, the Veil was torn and humankind was granted access to the Holy of Holies with the death of Jesus Christ on the cross.

We must ask Him to reveal Himself to us as never before. It is here He comes to us…the Veil torn that we might have access to His presence.

This Holy of Holies was where the priests came once a year for the purpose of sprinkling blood on the Mercy Seat in an effort to atone for the sins of the people for a year. It was where the physical evidence of the God of Israel lingered in the pillar of cloud by day and pillar of fire by night.

The Ark of the Covenant, housed behind the Veil, was constructed by specific design and direction given to Moses by God.

Exodus 25:22 contains the promise:

> "And there I will meet with thee, and I will commune with thee from above the mercy seat, from between the two cherubims which are upon the ark of the testimony, of all things which I will give thee in commandment unto the children of Israel."

When the tabernacle was completed, the Ark of the Covenant was placed in the Holy of Holies. A tabernacle without the Ark would have been just a badger skin tent. This Ark is significant in that it identifies God's desire to bring humanity into His presence. He didn't wait for man to come to Him; He took the first step and established the place and the plan. God started at the Ark of the Covenant and put the rest of the Wilderness Tabernacle in place. Man, on the other hand, in moving toward God had to start at the Brazen Altar and a place of repentance.

The High Priest was required to take off his usual priestly garments and replace them with holy garments designed just for that day, for that act of service.

THE PURPOSE, POWER, AND PATTERN

Today, we have direct access to Jesus Christ. No High Priest is required. The blood Jesus Christ shed on Calvary purchased for us freedom from sin and the trappings of the Law. When the spear pierced the side of Jesus Christ as He hung on Calvary's cross, the sun became dark, the earth shook, and according to Matthew 27:51, "the veil of the temple was rent in twain from the top to the bottom." Access was granted. No longer would the blood of bulls and goats be required. The Lamb was slain.

The Purpose of these final steps are to give us the boldness to approach His presence with faith. We are empowered, as we pray, to boldly step from the Altar of Incense, past the veil torn once and for all that day when Christ died for us all, and we can now boldly approach His throne.

The Power of these closing moments of praying through the Tabernacle Plan is the very essence of prayer in His presence. At this final juncture, our presence in His presence gives Kingdom power and authority into our hands through the prayers we pray in this holiest of Holy Places.

The Pattern is not for us to rush through these final steps but to linger as long as we need at the Altar of Incense, to take our time passing through the Veil to find ourselves in front of the Holy of Holies.

Just as the High Priest was required to change his clothes before going into the Holy of Holies, so you and I must rid ourselves of everything we might think would make us worthy in order to allow nothing but His righteousness to take us there. Jesus is our righteousness. When I come to Him, I come knowing that He is everything and I am nothing. It is here we find a place of fellowship and intimate communion. It is with holy reverence and awe we step beyond the rent veil into His presence.

Hebrews 4:16 reminds us, "Let us therefore come boldly unto the throne of grace that we may obtain mercy and find grace to help in the time of need." Then in Hebrews 13:5-6, we read, "for he hath said, I will never leave thee nor forsake thee...so that we may boldly say, The Lord is my helper and I will not fear what man shall do unto me."

The Ark of the Covenant, with its bloody Mercy Seat, is the most complete type and figure of the Lord Jesus Christ in his entire redemptive work. I believe the Ark represents the human heart, the deepest most intimate part of who you are. It is there the glory of God can take up residence and transform you and everything around you.

When we begin to live in this Holy of Holies dimension of prayer, we join our heart with the heart of God. It is then we will see His glory released in the earth, in our churches, in our communities, in our homes, and in our own hearts.

Here is our story of love and forgiveness found in Jesus Christ alone. He is our Mercy Seat – set forth to be the propitiation for us. "Herein is love, not that we loved God, but that he loved us, and sent his Son to be the propitiation for our sins" (I John 4:10). While the Tabernacle in the Wilderness was for the children of

Israel only, the rending of the Veil was done for all. "And he is the propitiation for our sins: and not for ours only, but also for the sins of the whole world" (I John 2:2).

There were three articles of significance stored in the Ark of the Covenant: a pot of manna, the rod of Aaron, and the two tables of the Law given to Moses. Jesus Christ is our ark, and we find in Him the bread of life. We find resurrection power in Him. The fruit and gifts of the Holy Ghost and the power and authority of Jesus name over all demonic forces, over all diseases, and over all sicknesses are now within our access. Rather than the law, Jesus has given us freedom from judgment and the liberty of the grace of God.

The Ark of the Covenant housed the glory of God. The bloody Mercy Seat, the presence of angels, and the promises of His word and His work are all there. There must be a manifestation of the Word operating in my life every day. We must, in our daily prayer time, make sure that we have walked through the Tabernacle Plan and have not stopped until we have spent time in the Holy of Holies where He can commune with us, and we can commune with Him in unhindered worship and adoration.

As an epistle "read of all men," we must declare to others what the Lord has done for me. We must, like Aaron's rod that budded, bring forth the fruit of the Spirit and the gifts of the Holy Spirit. The omer of manna had to be gathered every day. This tells us we can trust the Lord for everything we need!

When Solomon's Temple was destroyed, there was nothing mentioned in the Scriptures regarding the Ark. We do not know what became of it. It is certainly considered one of the greatest mysteries of all.

Yet, in truth, even in this it again fulfills a type of Jesus Christ – eternal and knowing no end.

In Revelation 11:19, John the Revelator said, "I saw it" but was his sight figurative or literal? We know not.

It is at the throne of God the blood speaks for us. There is no recorded prayer of Aaron for the Day of Atonement. He didn't have to speak because the blood speaks. The blood is a powerful force. When you repent and are baptized in His name, the blood eradicates your sins. The blood speaks for you. God placed the Mercy Seat over the Law, and the throne of judgment has become a throne of mercy and grace.

In this final segment of the journey through *Heaven on Earth,* I hope you have come to a fresh and perhaps new understanding of the work of the Tabernacle – and what it can mean in our lives today.

You can do it all in less than an hour; you can linger over each piece and spend a day in prayer. The important thing is that you,

Enter His gates with thanksgiving and his courts with praise.

Kneel at an Altar of true repentance and offer
yourself as a living sacrifice.

Daily wash yourself in His Word; let His word
teach you purity and holiness before God.

Pray for yourself and others as you discover
Jesus Christ to be wonderful, the wise counselor,
the mighty God, the everlasting father,
the prince of peace.

When you find yourself in the Holy Place,
keep the oil in your lamp burning brightly.

Pray for those who carry
the bread of life to the hungry and hurting.

Make sure the incense of worship is a daily
part of your offering to God.
Every day, make it a part of your purpose in prayer
to step behind the Veil into that realm where
the Shekinah glory of God fills your temple.

Remember, too, there was only one passageway into and out of the Tabernacle of Moses. You entered His courts with praise and thanksgiving. You exit the same way, though differently than when you came in. Your thanksgiving and praise as you leave the sanctuary of His presence are changed. You came in a sinner; you leave redeemed by His blood, anointed and empowered by His Holy Spirit.

Praying the Tabernacle
Heaven to Earth
will change your prayer life.
It will change your walk with God.
It will change your world.
It has mine.
Ever' Day!

EVER'
DAY
THE PRAYER GUIDE

EVER' DAY

The title of this section reflects a little bit of southern colloquialism. Though my dad was born in Indiana, he married a girl from Texas and ultimately spent almost seven of the nine decades of his life in the south, specifically in Alexandria, Louisiana. We speak "southern" here, and my Dad, while being very eloquent and often emphatic in his preaching and teaching, once in awhile allowed the influence of the place to be evidenced in this one phrase. He would talk about fasting every week, but when it came to prayer, it was something he did – and he taught us to do – "ever' day."

So, for this final segment of the book, where I will share with you the details of how he and I pray through the Tabernacle, it seemed only fitting that the section should be called "Ever' Day."

As we have said, the plan was not original to him. He was the one, though, who shared it with us. I can tell you from my own personal experience that it will revolutionize your personal prayer time when you institute this prayer pattern in your life "ever' day."

There will be parts of this section that will seem repetitive if you are reading the whole book from start to finish. However, this section is a tool to help you pray through the tabernacle. It will remind you of what you've read, learned, and already know. It will help you create a journal, of sorts, of your personal journeys as you pray "ever' day" through the Tabernacle Plan.

> "Who serve unto the example and shadow of
> heavenly things, as Moses was admonished of God
> when he was about to make the tabernacle:
> for, See, saith he, that thou make all things
> according to the pattern shewed to thee in the
> mount" (Hebrews 8:5).

The Tabernacle in the Wilderness provided the children of Israel with a specific place to come into the presence of Jehovah, a place of sacrifice and worship, a place of protection and direction. Just as that pattern shown to Moses in the mount brought the children of Israel into the presence of Jehovah, our own personal journey in prayer through that plan brings us into the presence of Almighty God.

The placement of the tent, its furnishings, and its furniture all were that "shadow of heavenly things" illustrating and demonstrating what is required to stand in the presence of God. The tabernacle reflects God's attributes and makes His blessings accessible to His people. The tabernacle creates for us as individuals a pattern – God's pattern – for us to follow in prayer that will usher us into His presence. It can be prayed in a prayer room or in your bedroom, in your living room, in your car, or in a garden. Just as the tabernacle of old was portable, so this prayer plan can be used in any setting.

The focus of the tabernacle was ultimately to reach the place where man could be in communion with the shekinah presence of Jehovah in the Holy of Holies. So it is our prayer through the Tabernacle Plan will ultimately lead us through thanksgiving, repentance, and the washing of the Word. It will then take us into a Holy Place in prayer where we can make our petitions known and make intercession for ourselves and others to ultimately move into the very presence of God "behind the Veil" where mercy and the miraculous reside.

The Tabernacle is a shadow of things in heaven. It is a "figure (of Him) who was to come...the Lord Jesus Christ " (Hebrews 9:9). It is symbolic of the Biblical plan of salvation for the New Testament church age. It is a powerful prayer pattern for all who are in Christ today. There are fifty chapters in the Bible given to the description, rituals, and meanings of it all: thirteen chapters of Exodus and Numbers, eighteen in Leviticus, two in Deuteronomy, and four in Hebrews. It has been observed that the Creation story is captured in thirty-one verses of the first chapter of Genesis. The tabernacle story from the instructions given to Moses on Mount Sinai through the final words concerning that Tabernacle in the New Testament is in well over ten times that number of verses.

Why pray this pattern? Can you even imagine a personal prayer life that when followed consistently will usher you into the presence of God? A prayer life that can happen to you, for you, in you, and through you every day? The tabernacle had significant places of washing, sacrifice, divine truth, protection, purpose, and ultimately the Holy of Holies, God's own presence. It is a plan, from Heaven to earth, for all of us to become what He has always had in mind for us to be – men and women of prayer and power in His presence.

Mark Batterson shared in an online devotional in 2012 entitled "The Outer Courts" the following observation:

"The Outer Courts are filled with distraction. It's
hard to hear. The Holy Place is still. And when you
get into the inner courts, all the other voices vying
for our attention are silenced" (Mark Batterson,
"Outer Courts," Mark Batterson (*blog)*, February 3,
2012, feedburner@markbatterson.com).

If we can, in our personal individual lives of prayer learn not to
be satisfied lingering in the Outer Courts, but rather to seek time
in the Holy of Holies, that place where the shekinah glory of God
is evidenced not just in our prayer but in our lives, it will make us
better people, better disciples of Christ, and ultimately better
disciple-makers.

More than anything else, I want to be known as a man who
has power in prayer. I will be a better husband and father,
grandfather and son because I am a man of prayer. I will be a more
compassionate pastor and a more passionate preacher if I am a man
of prayer. I will be the best kind of friend to saints and sinners
when I am a man of prayer. I will be a passionate disciple-maker
when I am a man of prayer. So it is I pray, imitating the example
of my father before me, "ever' day," following the Tabernacle Plan
into His presence, coming forth with power and authority that can
only come to rest on me there.

PRAYING
THE PLAN

SOME NOTES BEFORE BEGINNING PRAYING THE PLAN

Throughout the process of praying the Tabernacle Plan I utilize the practice of praying scriptures. If you've never done this before, it can sound difficult and intimidating. However, it is one of the simplest ways to invite the presence of God into your prayer time. When you pray His Word, especially when you pray the words aloud, there is power in His spoken Word that comes into your prayer time.

Here are two examples of how I "pray" the Psalms. Psalm 100:1-5 and an excerpt from Psalm 51 are below with the scriptural words in italics, followed by my words of prayer and/or praise. While it may seem easier to just read the words, let me assure you that there is an intensified power in the spoken and prayed Word. Read the scriptures and pray the prayers aloud.

As I begin my prayer time and seek entrance into His presence and admission into the tabernacle through the Entrance Gate, I will pray Psalm 100:1-5:

"Make a joyful noise unto the Lord, all ye lands."

> I come before You, Lord with a thankful heart. I want to praise and magnify Your name. I make a joyful noise unto You.

149

"Serve the Lord with gladness: come before his presence with singing."

Thank You for allowing me to serve you with gladness.
Thank you for allowing me to come before You with singing.

"Know ye that the Lord he is God: it is he that hath made us, and not we ourselves; we are his people, and the sheep of his pasture."

Thank You, Lord God, for making me and for allowing me to be Yours – a part of your people and a part of the sheep of your pasture.

"Enter into his gates with thanksgiving, and into his courts with praise: be thankful unto him, and bless his name."

I enter into Your gates today with thanksgiving for all You have done for me. I come into your courts with praise; You are a great and mighty God. I am thankful for all You have done and all You have given me. I bless Your name!

For the Lord is good; his mercy is everlasting; and his truth endureth to all generations.

I thank You, Lord, because You are good. I thank You for mercy that is everlasting. I thank You for truth that endures to all generations.

Several times a week I pray Psalm 51 as a part of my prayer at the Laver of Water, where I am seeking to be washed by the Word. Here is where I often pray through Psalm 51:9-15:

Hide thy face from my sins, and blot out all mine iniquities.

Oh, God, I am guilty of sin and iniquity. As much as I desire to walk before you in perfection, I find myself falling short. I am flawed. I am human. Like Paul admitted to the Romans, too often I do not do what I know I should do, and I do what I know I should not. (Romans 7:19). Hide Your face from my sins and blot out my iniquities.

Create in me a clean heart, O God;

Only You can make a perfect heart. Only You can truly know my heart. You promised through Isaiah that you would give us new hearts and new spirits. (Ezekiel 36:26). So take my heart today. Make it clean and holy before You.

And renew a right spirit within me.

Make my spirit right. Only You can correct what is wrong in me. Only You can heal what is broken. Renew a right spirit, one that comes from a clean heart that is focused on You. Don't let me become caught up in spirits of the age or entangled with the trappings of the uncommitted human spirit.

Cast me not away from thy presence; and take not thy holy spirit from me.

Your word tells us that all have sinned and fallen short of Your glory (Romans 3:23). I know I have sinned but I plead with You to allow me to once again feel your presence. Please, Lord, do not take Your Spirit from me. Grant forgiveness to my repentant heart.

Restore unto me the joy of thy salvation; and uphold me with thy free spirit.

Restore joy to me. Let me have a rejoicing heart and mind and soul. I know Your joy – the joy of the Lord – is my strength. Give me the joy of Your saving grace and unending mercy to me. Let Your free spirit uphold me.

Then will I teach transgressors thy ways; and sinners shall be converted unto thee.

> Let me teach those who have transgressed Your commandments and your ways; let me bring sinners to a place where they will be converted to You.

Deliver me from bloodguiltiness, O God, thou God of my salvation: and my tongue shall sing aloud of thy righteousness.

> Deliver me from bloodguiltiness, O God. I may not have physically killed anyone, but I may have said something to destroy someone's character. I may have said or done something to kill someone else's dreams. Deliver me from the weight and despair of my selfishness and my sinfulness. Deliver me from sins of omission and commission. You are the God who saves me! Let me sing of Your righteousness.

O Lord, open thou my lips; and my mouth shall shew forth thy praise.

> Today, Lord, open my lips today. Let the words I speak be words of praise and adoration to You. Let me speak words of hope and help to those I encounter today. Let everything I say and do show forth Thy praise. Let me speak words and sing songs that bring You glory and honor and praise!

As you pray through this Tabernacle Plan, you will find other scriptures and other opportunities to pray the Word. There are countless scriptures that can be applied at each stopping point on this prayer journey. Praying the Word is always appropriate. It always invites His presence in a unique and special way. He always responds when He hears your voice speaking His words. He longs for it ever' day.

THE SONGS OF THE TABERNACLE

A great singing voice and the ability to carry a tune with perfection is not required. After all, the Psalmist did say, "Make a joyful noise…" (Psalm 98:4). In your own heart and life, commit yourself to be the one who says, "I, even I, will sing unto the Lord; I will sing praise to the Lord God of Israel" (Judges 5:3).

Sometimes, as I am in prayer, moving through the tabernacle fixtures - praying at the Altar, the laver, the table - songs will come to mind. Sometimes it is the words of an old hymn; sometimes it is a current worship song. In either scenario, the songs become a part of my prayer. Listed throughout this "Ever' Day" section, you will find some of these songs with the artist noted for quick reference. At the end of the writing, Appendix A provides the full discography and reference for each of the songs.

While there is no scriptural indication there was singing in the Tabernacle, it is perfectly acceptable to make singing a part of your Tabernacle Prayer experience. The songs may change from day to day. You may not sing at the same point in your prayer journey. Some days you may sing a lot; other days you may not sing at all. The point is, if He gives you a song, do not be afraid to sing it!

THE
ENTRANCE
GATE

G. Anthony Mangun

We take this initial step into the Outer Court by worshipping the Almighty and true God. It is here we read or quote Scriptures of praise and worship. We sing songs of praise and worship. We adore Him. We bow before Him. As we desire to enter into the holiness of His presence, we understand we must first approach Him with thanksgiving and praise.

G. A. Mangun

The Entrance Gate was formed by four posts, symbolic of the four Gospels. Matthew and John were apostles. Mark and Luke were not, but they came in and substantiated what Matthew and John had written. The Jesus found in the Gospel accounts – the words penned by Matthew, Mark, Luke and John – is who we seek to know. You must make yourself responsible for knowing what is in those books.

Gentry A. Mangun

Before I can ask Him for anything, I thank Him for everything.

EVER' DAY
THE ENTRANCE GATE

There was only one point of entry into the Tabernacle of Moses. It was defined by four columns draped with a screen of finely twisted linen in a dramatic array of colors – blue, purple, and scarlet.

The four columns that held up the colorful curtains are symbolic of the four gospels. It is in these books that we discover who Jesus is and reasons to praise and thank Him. He is "the door." He is "the way, the truth, and the life." He is "the gate." He is the "Good Shepherd" leading us through life.

The colors of the curtains each have significance: blue for the deity of Christ (I Timothy 3:16), purple for royalty (Revelation 11:15), and scarlet for the shed blood of Jesus that redeems us.

We bring all things with us – as part of us – when we enter the Outer Court through the gate of thanksgiving and praise.

PRAYER FOCUS

The Psalmist David instructed us, in Psalm 100:4, to "enter into his gates with thanksgiving and into his courts with praise: Be thankful unto him, and bless his name."

Praying through the Tabernacle Plan begins with thanksgiving and praise. Pray the scriptures of praise and thanksgiving. Sing the songs. Be thankful from your heart for all things, using your own thoughts and words to lift Him up.

As I begin my prayer each day, I follow the instruction of the Psalmist David. I come through the gate proclaiming His greatness – giving thanks and praise for the mighty things He has done for me. I thank Him for the gifts He has given me. I thank Him for the works He has done.

SCRIPTURES

For the sake of this study and demonstration, I am including only four scriptures – two from the Old Testament and two from the New Testament. Get a good concordance and see how many great scriptures there are that incite us to praise and thanksgiving!

Psalms 150:1: *Praise ye the LORD. Praise God in his sanctuary: praise him in the firmament of his power.*

Psalms 106:1: *Praise ye the LORD. O give thanks unto the LORD; for [he is] good: for his mercy [endureth] forever.*

Hebrews 13:15: *By him therefore let us offer the sacrifice of praise to God continually, that is, the fruit of [our] lips giving thanks to his name.*

I Thessalonians 5:18: *In every thing give thanks: for this is the will of God in Christ Jesus concerning you.*

SONGS

"Praise Him!" (Traditional)

"Praise The Lord" (Russ Taff with The Imperials)

"Waymaker" (Kara V. Williams with The Pentecostals of Alexandria Choir)

"Majesty" (Truth)

"Total Praise" (Mickey Mangun)

THINGS FOR WHICH I DAILY GIVE THANKS

Jesus Christ – God, manifest in flesh, come to earth to save us

Salvation and The Word

Family – I call each of them by name, pausing to be thankful for particular things about them for which I am especially thankful; "Thank You, Jesus, for giving me a wonderful godly wife, an anointed woman of prayer and the Word."

Friends – I call them by name, just like my family.

Physical Health

Financial Blessings

Creature Comforts (home, car, etc.)

Food/Water

Shelter/Clothing

Work

MY PRAYER

Holy Heavenly Father, I enter into Your gates with thanksgiving. I approach this entrance into Your presence with praise. I love You and adore You. I worship You with every breath that is within me. I bow before You. I proclaim your greatness. Like the Psalmist David, I want to make Your praise glorious (Psalm 66:2)!

You are the Almighty and all powerful King of Kings and Lord of Lords. There is no god like You. You are the creator of all things. You are the giver of life. You are the alpha and omega – the beginning and the end of all things.

I proclaim your greatness. I thank You for everything You have done. I thank You for every good and perfect gift You have given me. From the depths of my soul – with all of my heart and mind and soul and strength – I thank You, Jesus. You are great and greatly to be praised!

After an initial time of praise and thanksgiving, I work my list – thanking Him for family and friends and health, etc..

MY PRAYER AT THE ENTRANCE GATE

_____

_____

_____

_____

_____

_____

_____

_____

_____

_____

_____

_____

_____

_____

_____

THE BRAZEN ALTAR

G. Anthony Mangun

Our Altars must always be bigger than our arks. In the Tabernacle of Moses, the Brazen Altar was not only the largest piece of furniture, it was so large that every other piece of Tabernacle furniture could have been packed into it. It's not a step that can be skipped over or rushed through. Jesus Christ died to purchase our salvation. We must seek Him diligently, asking for forgiveness for all of our sins. We must cry out in repentance before Him. We must offer ourselves to Him unreservedly. As He submitted Himself to the cross, so must we submit ourselves to this Altar of sacrifice. We lay down everything we are in order to allow Him to burn out of us anything that is not like Him, anything that is not pleasing to Him. Paul said, "I die daily" (I Corinthians 15:31). This is where that happens. It is a place of death and dying. It is the place of true repentance.

G. A. Mangun

Ask God to burn out everything in you. Ask God to clean you. You are a holy nation. Present your body/soul/spirit in true repentance. I ask God to cleanse me. I ask God to burn out everything in me that is not like Him.

Gentry A. Mangun

This place – the largest piece of furniture in the whole Tabernacle – reminds me of how vast the grace of God actually is.

EVER' DAY
THE BRAZEN ALTAR

As we enter the Outer Court, the first stop is the Brazen Altar. This is where in the Tabernacle of Moses, the sacrifices were offered. Whether you were offering the sacrifice of a bull or lamb, a turtledove or pigeon – whether your offering was meal and incense – your first stop after you entered through the Entrance Gate was the Brazen Altar.

It was not a pleasant place to linger, yet it was required. Ordained by the Jehovah God of Israel, the systematic sacrifice of animals was central to the hearts and lives of the children of Israel. One writer observed, "the unceasing sacrifice of animals, and the never-ending glow of fire at the Altar of sacrifice…(leaves) no doubt God was burning into the hearts of every man, an awareness of his own sin" (bible_history.com/The Sacrifices).

It is at the Brazen Altar we confess our sins and repent for every sinful wrong. "Ever' Day" we must find a place of true repentance before God. It is at this Brazen Altar that we ourselves become the sacrifice offered. Paul wrote, "I beseech you therefore, brethren, by the mercies of God, that ye present your bodies a living sacrifice, holy, acceptable unto God, which is your reasonable service" (Romans 12:1). To the Corinthians, he wrote of dying daily (I Corinthians 15:31). Before we can progress on the rest of our journey through the Tabernacle, we must confess our sins and repent. We must offer ourselves as that living sacrifice to Him.

Prayer Focus

This Brazen Altar is the place where I cry out as a sinner in need of a Savior and ask God to forgive me for every sin and wrong-doing. It is here I ask His forgiveness for my selfishness and self-centeredness. It is here I repent for my prejudices and my pride. I admit there is nothing good in me except Him.

This place that is symbolic of the cross of Christ, where He was the Lamb, slain for my sin, I find my own place of repentance and death to self. Too often, I can fool myself into believing I am without sin or wrong-doing. It is here I come face to face with the fact that I am guilty of wrong-doing, sinful thoughts, and perhaps even sinful deeds. A continually repentant heart is foremost.

Scriptures
Ezekiel 18:21: *But if the wicked will turn from all his sins that he hath committed, and keep all my statutes, and do that which is lawful and right, he shall surely live, he shall not die.*
Proverbs 28:13: *He that covereth his sins shall not prosper: but whoso confesseth and forsaketh [them] shall have mercy.*
Acts 3:19: *Repent ye therefore, and be converted, that your sins may be blotted out, when the times of refreshing shall come from the presence of the Lord;*
II Peter 3:9: *The Lord is not slack concerning his promise, as some men count slackness; but is longsuffering to us-ward, not willing that any should perish, but that all should come to repentance.*

Songs
"Give Us Clean Hands" (Chris Tomlin)
"I Surrender All" (Traditional)
"Just As I Am" (Traditional)
"Fill Me" (Martha Munizzi)
"I Need You More" (Kim Walker-Smith and Jesus Culture)

THINGS I PRAY AT THE BRAZEN ALTAR

I acknowledge I am a sinner because "all have sinned and come short of the glory of God" (Romans 3:23).

I repent of my sins of omission – things I should have said or done but didn't.

I repent of my sins of commission – things I should not have said or done.

Let none of the works of the flesh in Galatians 5:19-21 be found in me. Let the fruit of the Spirit be present in me.

MY PRAYER

Dear Lord Jesus, as I approach the Brazen Altar, I am struck by the fact that it symbolizes the cross where You died for me. You were beaten and bruised. You suffered stripes. You were brutally crucified. You shed Your blood. You died. For me. You did it all that I might have redemption from sin.

So I bring to You my repentant heart. I repent of everything I have done that was not pleasing to You. I repent of everything I have said that was not pleasing to You. I beg your forgiveness for my sins of omission and my sins of commission.

I lay myself on this Altar of repentance and offer myself to You as a living sacrifice. Take from me all that is not like You. Remove from me everything that is not pleasing to you. I join the Psalmist David in crying out to you, "Create in me a clean heart, O God; and renew a right spirit within me" (Psalms 51:10).

Forgive me for any unforgiveness I have carried in my heart. Forgive me of jealousy, envy, strife, murmuring, backbiting and complaining – everything sinful and not pleasing to You found in me. I repent before You for wrongful words and deeds.

I may know some aspects of my nature. However, my heart is deceitful (Jeremiah 17:9). I can think I know it and do not. So I ask you to search me and cleanse me. Burn out everything in me that is not a part of Your plan for my life. Let me surrender my heart and life to You as a living sacrifice. You, O Lord, are my consuming fire (Hebrews 12:29).

My Prayer At The Brazen Altar

_____

_____

_____

_____

_____

_____

_____

_____

_____

_____

_____

_____

_____

_____

THE LAVER OF WATER

G. Anthony Mangun

I will never forget when as a child I was baptized in your name. February 7, 1957 my life was totally changed, and you washed me in Your name and in Your blood. Now, these decades later, after having laid myself on the Altar of repentance and sacrifice, I ask You to cleanse me again. The Word cleanses and washes me. I am so thankful for that Word that is "the lamp unto my feet and light unto my path" (Psalm 119:105). I must be washed with the Word.

G. A. Mangun

The priests went to the Laver. The purpose was to cleanse and sanctify themselves for service. So I pray, "Sanctify me. Cleanse me of anything that would be of a hindrance to Your divine plan. Wash me. Make me like you so that the reflection I see will not just be me – but will ultimately be you in me.

Gentry A. Mangun

This reflecting pool is where I pause to make sure that the reflection is ultimately Jesus Christ not Gentry Mangun.

EVER' DAY
THE LAVER OF WATER

When the priests left the Brazen Altar and approached the Laver of Water, they were able to see a double reflection of themselves. They saw themselves reflected in the water and then in the basin itself. When you and I approach the Laver of Water as we pray this Tabernacle Prayer Plan, God shows us two important things about ourselves. He shows us who we really are, and He shows us who we are in Him. We see very clearly what we are and what we are becoming as He imparts His Word to us.

In Ephesian 5:25-27, tucked in with the instruction to husbands to love their wives as Christ loved the church is this important phrase: "that he might sanctify and cleanse it (the church) with the washing of water by the word" It is at this Laver of Water, empowered by the Word, that we find sanctification and cleansing.

PRAYER FOCUS

James 1 tells us to "be doers of the Word." We cannot just listen to it or read it and not apply it. Jesus said, "If ye continue in my Word, then ye are my disciples indeed" (John 8:31). It is only in the Word, by doing the Word and continuing in the Word, that we become His disciples.

Praying the Word becomes our washing. As we read various scriptures and claim the promises of God, we are being washed by the power of His Word.

When I pray and say, "By your stripes I am healed…" (I Peter 2:24) the power of that Word washes over me and brings with it both faith and healing.

When I pray, "Let nothing separate me from you, Lord…" and claim the words of Romans 8:39, I am washed by the Word and accept the power of His promise for me.

SCRIPTURES
Psalm 51:2: *Wash me thoroughly from mine iniquity, and cleanse me from my sin.*
Isaiah 55: 11: *So shall my Word be that goeth forth out of my mouth: it shall not return unto me void but it shall accomplish that which I please, and it shall prosper in the thing where to I sent it.*
Hebrews 4:12: *For the word of God is quick, and powerful, and sharper than any two-edged sword, piercing even to the dividing asunder of soul and spirit, and of the joints and marrow, and is a discerner of the thoughts and intents of the heart.*
II Timothy 3:16: *All scripture is given by inspiration of God, and is profitable for doctrine, for reproof, for correction, for instruction in righteousness.*

SONGS
"Word of God Speak" (Mercy Me)
"Water Grave" (Mickey Mangun)
"I Want to Be Holy" (Randy Phillips)
"Take My Life (Holiness)" (Micah Stampley)

THINGS I PRAY AT THE LAVER OF WATER
Cleanse my hands, my heart, my mind.
Let me be holy as He is holy.
Removal of anything that is not like Him.

MY PRAYER

Heavenly Father, I come now to this Laver of Water. I ask You to cleanse me by the power of your Word. Let your Word speak to me and wash me from all sin and iniquity. David asked and answered the question "who will stand in his Holy Place?" in Psalm 24. I ask You to give me clean hands and a pure heart. I ask you to protect me and keep me from vanity and deceitfulness. I seek your blessing and righteousness here in this place of washing.

Let me become who Your Word tells me I can be. Remove condemnation from me (Romans 8:1). Let me understand and walk in my holy calling (II Timothy 1:9). Let me remember I am a child of God (Romans 8:16). I am forgiven (Colossians 1:13). I am redeemed (Psalms 31:5). I have been set apart for Your service (Psalm 4:3). You have purchased me, and I am Yours (I Corinthians 6:19, 20)

Your Word promises Your peace will keep my heart and mind through Christ Jesus (Philippians 4:7). Let nothing separate me from You (Romans 8:39).

My Prayer At The Laver of Water

_____

_____

_____

_____

_____

_____

_____

_____

_____

_____

_____

_____

_____

_____

THE HOLY PLACE

G. Anthony Mangun
These Five Pillars afford me the privilege of entering into the Holy Place of God. It is where I first encounter who He is.
He is Wonderful. (I often sing "Wonderful! Wonderful! Jesus is to me) He is my Counselor. I seek His wisdom, and He gives me insight. He is the Mighty God. There is no other god like Him. He is my everlasting Father. He loves me and cares for me and supplies my needs. He is my Prince of Peace. He gives me that peace that passes understanding.

G. A. Mangun
Jesus was in the church in the wilderness. His divine nature and attributes are revealed in the Five Pillars of the Entrance to the Holy Place.

Gentry A. Mangun
No matter what I'm going through, God has an attribute that will see me through. He is Wonderful, He is my wisest counselor, my mighty God, my everlasting Father and my Prince of Peace. He is everything I need, and He is more than enough for every one of life's situations.

EVER' DAY
THE HOLY PLACE

After entering the gateway of praise and thanksgiving and lingering at the Altar of sacrifice of self and offering a repentant heart, we moved to the Laver of Water to be washed by His Word. Now we find ourselves at the entrance to the Holy Place.

This is where we find the five pillars and the drapes that mark this entrance. There's no biblical connection between the entrance to the Holy Place and the descriptive names of God Isaiah penned in Isaiah 9:6. However, for my father, it seemed to be a good connect point. The revealed nature of God seemed a natural fit to this next step of entering into the place of holy things.

PRAYER FOCUS

As we focus on Him as Wonderful, Counselor, the Mighty God, the Everlasting Father, the Prince of Peace, we pray for these things from Him for ourselves and those around us. It is here I pray for him to make me ever mindful of how wonderful He is to me. I never want to miss the wonder of His presence in my life. I bring Him the things I need His direction about for He is a wise counselor and wants to direct my steps. I bring to Him the situations in my life that need Him to act with might and power. I also bring my personal needs, the needs of my heart, to my loving, benevolent, and everlasting Father. For all my turmoil, for the things I struggle with and for the things in my life that have brought stress and strife, I cry to the Prince of Peace for His peace in my life. I pray, too, these same things over my friends and family.

SCRIPTURES

Psalm 40:5: *Many, O Lord my God, are thy wonderful works which thou hast done, and thy thoughts which are to us-ward: they cannot be reckoned up in order unto thee: if I would declare and speak of them, they are more than can be numbered.*

Isaiah 63:16: *Thou, O Lord, art our father, our redeemer; thy name is from everlasting.*

John 16:23: *Verily, verily, I say unto you, Whatsoever ye shall ask the Father in my name, he will give it you.*

John 14:27: *Peace I leave with you, my peace I give unto you: not as the world giveth, give I unto you. Let not your heart be troubled, neither let it be afraid.*

SONGS

"His Name is Wonderful" (The Imperials)
"Because of Who You Are" (Vicki Yohe)
"Mighty God" (Trent Corey)
"Good, Good Father" (Chris Tomlin)
"Peace Speaker" (Cynthia McKellar-Dubois with the Pentecostals of Alexandria Choir)

LIST OF THINGS I PRAY AS I ENTER THE HOLY PLACE

Things about which I need counsel and direction
Things on which I need Him to move in a mighty way
The personal needs only a father can meet
The areas of my life that need peace

MY PRAYER

Jesus Christ, You are wonderful. You are wonderful in my life! There is no God like you – what a wonder you are! You are my wonderful Savior, my wonderful friend!

You are my Counselor. I want Your mind to be in me.

Counsel me. I want to be a better husband. I want to be a better father. Counsel my family. Give direction to my wife and to my children and grandchildren. Give Your direction to my mother. Let my family always know Your ways and follow Your pathways.

I pray for our pastoral staff and their families. Counsel us all that we might know how to care for the sheep of Your pasture.

I thank You, Lord, for the professional counselors You've sent to us. Walk with them and give them Your wise counsel as they address the unique needs of your people.

Lord Jesus, speak into our lives that we will all know how to handle the life You have given us. Let each one know what to do and what to say. Give us Your wisdom and teach us how to lead Your people home.

You are my mighty God! I thank You that I know Your name and the power that is in Your name. Thank You for showing me the truth of who You are. Thank you for revealing to me that You are One; "hear O Israel, the Lord our God, the Lord is one...\" (Deuteronomy 6:4) and the words of Jesus, "I and my Father are one" (John 10:30). You are the mighty God and there is no God like You. I am so thankful You are MY God – not just any god. You are Almighty and all powerful!

There is no Father like You. Be a father to those who are fatherless among us. I pray for those who have felt the pain and condemnation of divorce and for those children with absent fathers – I ask that You care for them and nourish them as only a heavenly Father can. I pray for You to be a loving Father to those who are in our Grace House and House of Mercy. I pray for You to bless our sweet Overcomers that come every Sunday in wheelchairs and live every day with the limitations of their bodies and minds. I thank You for the good father You blessed my life with. I thank You for all good fathers. I also ask You to become the Good Father that was never known to those who were abused by their fathers. Heal them and give them new understanding of Your Word and Your love for them. Be our Everlasting Father.

I pray for peace. In the name of Jesus, I speak peace into my life. I speak peace into my wife and children. I speak peace

177

into the leadership of this church. I speak peace into the POA congregation. I speak peace into us all – into our lives, our homes, and our marriages. I speak peace into the lives of our young people. Let them know that if they will stand for righteousness, You will give them the peace that passes understanding. I speak peace into our children.

Bring peace to our city, our state, our nation. Bring peace to the nation of Israel.

Forever be our Prince of Peace.

My Prayer As I Enter The Holy Place

THE GOLDEN CANDLESTICK

G. ANTHONY MANGUN

As I approach the Golden Candlestick, I ask the Lord to fill me with the Holy Ghost. I ask Him to set me afire, and make me a flame! Give me light and purity. Let the unction of the Holy Ghost be what moves and directs me. It is here I seek His guidance and direction for each day. I am Spirit-filled; I must be Spirit-led. Let me be light in this dark world.

G. A. MANGUN

Let the light of the Holy Ghost shine on me. Give me a revelation not just of who you are but also of who I am and who I am in you. At the Golden Candlestick, by the light of its fire, I read Revelation and pray through those Seven Churches of Revelation. Let each of their revelations be restored to me again.

GENTRY A. MANGUN

This is one of my favorite places to linger in my prayer through the Tabernacle. What is God's direction for me? This is where I pray for God to lead me, direct me, and to shine His light on my life and my ministry. To walk in the Spirit . . . to be in the Spirit . . .is to walk in His light.

EVER' DAY
THE GOLDEN CANDLESTICK

The curtains and skins prevented the entrance of any natural light into the Holy Place. The Golden Candlestick was the only source of light in the Holy Place besides the possible glow of burning incense at the Altar. However, the light – the oil in the candlestick – was to never go out. The priests were charged with the daily responsibility of making sure the oil in the lampstand was fresh and full, and that the fire would never go out.

For us today, the infilling of the Holy Spirit of God is just as needed. We must be full of His Spirit. We must walk in His light and be the light to the world in which we live.

PRAYER FOCUS

As we stand at the Golden Candlestick, we are tasked with the duty of keeping the lampstand full of oil. So our prayer is, first and foremost, that God fill us with the Holy Spirit. Let Your Holy Spirit consume and fill us. Let the oil of anointing flow through us and fill every open aspect of our lives with Your holy Sprit.

It is a place of illumination. So we pray for His light to shine on us and others. It is here we are reminded that He is the light and that, as He fills us, we are also the light of the world.

It is by His light we are led to others who need Him. It is here in His light that we come to understand the revelations He is speaking to us individually.

It is in the light of the Golden Candlestick we seek the unction and anointing of the Holy Ghost in our lives. We are Spirit-filled and are seeking, in the light of this Holy Place, to be Spirit-led.

SCRIPTURES
Psalm 27:1: *The LORD is my light and my salvation; whom shall I fear? the LORD is the strength of my life; of whom shall I be afraid?*
Isaiah 60:1: *Arise, shine; for thy light is come, and the glory of the LORD is risen upon thee.*
Matthew 5:14: *Ye are the light of the world...*
Ephesians 5:8: *For ye were sometimes darkness, but now are ye light in the Lord: walk as children of light:*

SONGS
"Daystar" (Jason Crabb)
"Welcome, Holy Spirit" (Mark Condon)
"Carrier" (Jared Anderson)
"Oceans (Where Feet May Fail)" (Hillsong United)
"Spirit of the Living God" (Traditional)
"He Leadeth Me" (The Martins)

THINGS I PRAY AT THE GOLDEN LAMPSTAND
I pray for light and direction,
for my darkness – illuminate and give me understanding about situations in my life.
for my life – let me walk in ordered steps. Lead me to lost and hurting people that need to see You in me.
for my family – let each member of my family walk in Your light. Let them ever be filled with your Spirit.
for the church – let every member of our church family walk in the light and live in the light that comes only from You.
Let there be an outpouring of Your Spirit in our church, our city, and our community.
Let there be an outpouring of Your Spirit in the world. Bring

Your light into countries without missionaries and into cities and towns across America that are in spiritual darkness.

MY PRAYER

I need to be baptized today with the Holy Ghost and fire. Let the oil of Your presence flow over me, through me, and fill me. Baptize me with a fresh touch of Holy Ghost and fire. Let the oil of Your Spirit and anointing flow. I pray, Lord, that You will let Your light shine on me.

I take time today to stop and tend the fire and oil of these candlesticks as the priests did twice a day. Help me cleanse the details of my life. Let nothing remain in me that hinders a free flow of Your Spirit in my life.

I pray the gifts of Your Spirit will find free operation in our church. I pray our church will become, as never before, that "city set on a hill." Help me to let the light of Your presence never flicker or fade. Let the men and women I see and interact with daily, as well as those who come in and out of my life, see good works and know that I am full of the oil of the Holy Ghost. Let the power of Your Spirit flow through me. Let the light shine.

I ask you, dear Lord, today, to let Your light shine on each member of my family. I pray for them to see You clearly. I pray for them to live lives full of the Holy Ghost and for their every step to be directed by you. I plead with you that none of us would ever allow the candle of Your Spirit to go out in any of our lives. Direct my steps, today, Lord. Let me go where I am supposed to go. Let me encounter those people who need to see Your light in me.

Let those who bring the Gospel to others around the world – at home and abroad – be bright beacons of hope and life to their lost worlds. Let someone go and bring light to cities, towns, and countries in spiritual darkness. Give me supernatural life – and supernatural light – as I walk in the Spirit.

My Prayer At The Golden Lampstand

_____

_____

_____

_____

_____

_____

_____

_____

_____

_____

_____

_____

_____

_____

THE TABLE
OF
SHEWBREAD

G. ANTHONY MANGUN

At the Table of Shewbread, I speak the Word and claim its promises. I pray over the pastoral staff and all of those who carry the Word . . . everyone from Sunday School teachers to full-time missionaries. I pray for revival around the world. I pray for Jerusalem.

G. A. MANGUN

The shewbread is the Word of the Lord. It is a powerful thing. The worlds were framed by His Word. God, anoint me with a revelation of Your Word. Give me a "rhema" from your "logos." Give me a message from your word. I pray for missionaries and ministers at home and abroad. Grant us a sovereign move of God in our personal lives, in our churches and in our ministries.

GENTRY A. MANGUN

There is power in the Word and in the prayed Word of God. It is here I pray for all of those who handle the Word of God whether by teaching, preaching, or personal testimony. I pray for my own "rhema," as my grandfather called it. I need my own personal word from the Lord, and here is where I seek it.

EVER' DAY
THE TABLE OF SHEWBREAD

There are two components at the next stop on our journey through the Tabernacle Plan: the Table and the Shewbread that rested upon it. The Shewbread itself was symbolic of the Word of God. The table is, for the sake of this prayer plan, a symbol or reminder in our prayer of those who carry the Gospel.

Jesus was the both the bread of life and the Word of God made flesh. His word is the bread of heaven. Eternal life is found in the Word.

On the Sabbath each week, the twelve loaves of unleavened bread were covered with frankincense and placed on the table by the designated priest. The Word, whether preached or taught or spoken, must be fresh. It follows suit that those who handle the bread should be clean and holy, walking worthy of their calling.

PRAYER FOCUS

The place of the showbread, both table and bread, is a place where prayer is offered for the lost among us – those hungry for the bread of life. It is where we pray for the Word to go forth without reservation or limitation. We pray anointing and power for those who are carrying the Gospel to the world through ministry of the Word.

This is where the power of praying the Word can be demonstrated as you find scriptures to match and meet the needs of those for whom you pray. We know that "it is not his will that any should perish" (II Peter 3:9) as we pray for lost souls to hear the Gospel message.

SCRIPTURES

Deuteronomy 8:16: *Who fed thee in the wilderness with manna, which thy fathers knew not, that he might humble thee, and that he might prove thee, to do thee good at thy latter end...*

Nehemiah 9:20: *Thou gavest also thy good spirit to instruct them, and withheldest not thy manna from their mouth, and gavest them water for their thirst.*

John 6:35: *And Jesus said unto them, I am the bread of life; he that cometh to me shall never hunger; and he that believeth on me shall never thirst.*

John 6:51: *I am the living bread which came down from heaven; if any man eat of this bread, he shall live forever; And the bread that I will give is my flesh, which I will give for the life of the world.*

SONGS

"Word of God Speak" (Mercy Me)
"Lord Prepare Me" (RandyRothwell)
"Breathe" (Michael W. Smith)
"God of This City" (Chris Tomlin)

THINGS I PRAY AT THE TABLE OF SHEWBREAD

Speak the Word; Pray the Word
Lead me to Scriptures to meet my needs
Daily Bread
Right words to speak
Pastoral staff and local church ministries
Churches around the country and world
Home and Foreign Missionaries (by name and/or by country)

MY PRAYER

Lord, I thank You for every promise in Your Word that is mine. That those promises are "yea" and "amen" (II Corinthians 1:20).

I thank You that no weapon formed against me will prosper, and no words spoken against me will matter (Isaiah 54:17).

I thank You for Your promise that when we lay hands on the sick "they shall recover" (Mark 16:18).

I thank You for your promise of "perfect peace" to those who trust You, and who keep their minds and hearts turned toward You (Isaiah 26:3).

I pray for every preacher who preaches the Word. I pray that they would be anointed and that their minds would be quickened.

I pray for church leaders. Let the light from the Candlestick shine and illuminate Your Word fresh and new to them.

I plead the blood over the preachers that I pastor and over my pastor friends.

I pray over our North American Missionaries. These are the men and women who left friends and families, nice homes and good churches to go into unchurched areas and take the bread of life. I pray for the bivocational pastors – those who are working full-time jobs in secular workplaces while devoting additional moments to bringing in a church for the Kingdom of God. I pray for God to give physical, emotional, and spiritual strength and renewal to each one of these ministers and families of these Kingdom builders. (Sometimes I get a map and pray state-by-state for North America and also for Canada.)

I pray for each of our world missionaries and AIM workers and others involved in world missions. It is here I often pray around the globe, calling names of the missionaries in prayer. I pray that God would give for these men and women who are holding the bread for their country keen insight into reaching the people of their regions. I pray for the revival of the nations.

I pray for the nation of Israel. I pray for the city of Jerusalem. I pray for God to bless His people and His nation. I pray for peace to come to that city (Psalm 122:6).

I pray for our pastors, missionaries, evangelists, and church leaders around the world to be given wisdom and knowledge. I ask God to lead and guide each of us into all truth.

I pray for God's protection over our people and our leaders – that the plots of terrorism would be thwarted. I pray for those who would wreak terror on us and ask that God instead bring someone into their individual lives who would share with them the message of the one true God and the only bread of life. Let the hatred and rage that motivates them be overwhelmed with God's pure love for them.

I pray for church. I pray for our Sunday School teachers and ministry leaders. I pray for those who are teaching Bible studies in homes and at various locations around our community. I pray for the living Word, that bread of life, to bring life to the lost and hurting in our area.

I pray anointing, wisdom, and spiritual insight into the Word for everyone in our congregation who shares the Word in any capacity. I pray for the Word to come alive in the hearts and lives of everyone in our congregation – and community – who reads the Word and hears the Word. It shall not return void (Isaiah 55:11)!

My Prayer At The Table of Shewbread

THE ALTAR
OF
INCENSE

G. Anthony Mangun

It is at this Altar of incense, inside the Holy Place, I intercede in prayer. I intercede for my church. I intercede for my family. I plead the blood over them. I stand in the gap for them. I stand as an intercessor for my church.

G. A. Mangun

This Altar is where I offer up the sacrifice of prayer and praise. I ask God to let me offer three things: the incense to offer up praise, prayer and worship. There are various incenses. Some you find in the mountain, and some you find in the valley. You will find the incense you offer is part of where you are in your walk with God. The people smelled the incense as it was offered.

Gentry A. Mangun

I worship God from the depths of my heart and soul. I intercede for my family, for my church, and for the ministers and ministries of our church. I plead the blood over us all.

EVER' DAY
The Altar of Incense

When you step into the Holy Place, the Golden Candlestick is to your left and the Table of Shewbread is to your right. In front of you, in the reflective light of the Golden Candlestick you see the Altar of Incense. This is the place where the sweet-smelling incense was offered by the priests every day. Fire on this Altar came from the Altar of sacrifice. There must be repentance before there can be praise and worship. It is also a place of intercession. It is the place where fresh incense – mixed every day – was offered up to God as a morning and evening sacrifice.

It is here at this Altar we make our petitions to God known and learn the power of praying "in the Spirit" (Ephesians 6:18). It is also where we discover the strength and power of worshiping "in Spirit and in truth" (John 4:24).

PRAYER FOCUS

We offer our personal praise and worship in the Spirit. We pray and intercede before God's throne for the needs of others. This is where we bring our personal needs and the needs of our family members and friends to God for His intervention.

It is here at this Altar of Incense where the prayers that bring spiritual breakthrough and divine intervention are prayed.

SCRIPTURES

Psalm 141:2: *Let my prayer be set forth before thee as incense; and the lifting up of my hands as the evening sacrifice.*

Jeremiah 17:26: *And they shall come from the cities of Judah, and from the places about Jerusalem, and from the land of Benjamin, and from the plain, and from the mountains, and from the south, bringing burnt offerings, and sacrifices, and meat offerings, and incense, and bringing sacrifices of praise, unto the house of the Lord.*

Hebrews 13:10: *We have an Altar…*

Hebrews 13:15: *By him therefore let us offer the sacrifice of praise to God continually, that is, the fruit of our lips giving thanks to his name.*

SONGS

"Hear Us From Heaven" (Jared Anderson)
"Ask" (BJ Putnam)
"Offering (I Bring an Offering of Worship to My King)" (Paul Baloche)
"I Worship You Almighty God" (Don Moen)
"Like Incense (Sometimes By Step)" (Hillsong)

THINGS I PRAY AT THE ALTAR OF INCENSE

Personal needs
Family members
Church family with special needs
The needs of the Body of Christ

MY PRAYER

Almighty God, I bring before You today my personal sacrifice of praise and worship. I thank You for every blessing. I thank You, too, for every trial and test. I thank You for allowing me to walk with You and for the assurance that You are walking with me.

Today, I come to this Altar of Incense, and I intercede for the needs of my family.

I intercede for the needs of the members of this church.

I intercede for this community and for our great Bayou state.

I plead the blood over them. I stand in the gap for them all. I stand as an intercessor for this church.

For our families and for our children, I plead Your blood and intercede before You.

I intercede for our marriages and family relationships. Lord, You alone know where there are needs for healing and restoration, and You alone are able to bring those things.

I intercede for the power of our church to not be diminished. I pray for unity to remain and for anointing and blessing to rest on us. I intercede against those who would sow disunity and discord among us.

I intercede on behalf of the great people I pastor. You know their needs even better than I do. You alone are able to supply those needs, to move on their behalf.

I intercede before Your throne, asking for revival to come as never before. Work in our lives and let us lift You up in such a way that all men are drawn to you. I intercede for those who do not know You yet. I intercede for those who have known You before but drifted away.

Lord Jesus, I offer up the incense you require of us all. I mix together the ingredients and offer them to You with my worship – fresh and new every morning and every evening. I ask You to give me the "skill of the apothecary" (Exodus 30:35) as I mix the ingredients for the incense from my heart and life.

Let my worship not be or become stale. Do not let there be flies in the ointment to spoil and destroy it (Ecclesiastes 10:1).

I prostrate myself before You. You are King of Kings and Lord of Lords. From the depths of my soul, I worship You.

My Prayer At The Altar Of Incense

_____

_____

_____

_____

_____

_____

_____

_____

_____

_____

_____

_____

_____

THE
HOLY
OF
HOLIES

G. ANTHONY MANGUN
This final step of the Tabernacle Plan brings us into the shekinah presence of God – the place where His presence dwells. We step through the torn Veil into a place of mercy. I have not committed a sin that the Mercy Seat will not cover. My sins were left at the Altar. Mercy is with me everywhere I go. There is manna here. Give me a desire and hunger for your Word and Your presence as never before. Let the Word of God give me strength. The tablets are here. I pray the 10 Commandments – the first five are "unto God" and the last five things are promises of what I will not do. Aaron's Rod is here . . . a rod of authority. It is here I take authority over everything that has come against me. It is here I war in the Spirit and pray victory into existence.

G. A. MANGUN
I thank God I am inside the covenant. I'm covered with His mercy and His blood, and His angels are over me. There are woven angels on the inside ceiling of the Holy Place . . .God has, in this Holy of Holies, given us access to angels.

GENTRY A. MANGUN
At the Veil – the pillars of Matthew, Mark, Luke, and John – I identify my desire to live my life as Jesus lived His. As I step into the Holy of Holies, I want to be saturated with His presence. In His presence, I bring my petitions before Him and find His favor.

EVER' DAY
THE HOLY OF HOLIES

As we reach this final step in our journey through the Tabernacle Plan of prayer, we find ourselves again facing four pillars or posts. These, like the ones at the Entrance Gate are symbolic of the four Gospel writers: Matthew, Mark, Luke, and John. It is a reminder that, in order for us to know Him, we must study the Gospels and the accounts of who He was when He walked among men.

Also here, we step through the Veil that separated the Holy of Holies from the Holy Place. Just a small ten by twenty room, this is where the presence of the Most High God is found. To reach this place of His presence is the culmination of our journey. Every previous step has been bringing us closer and closer to His presence.

The small space is overwhelmed by the Ark of the Covenant. The Ark with the Mercy Seat sprinkled with blood reminds us that mercy is always above the Law. It is in the ark itself that we see the manna – and are reminded of God's promise of provision. We see Aaron's rod that budded and are reminded that we can pray with the authority of God in this place. It is where the ten commandments remind us of God's unchangeable standards for our lives.

PRAYER FOCUS

When we reach the Holy of Holies, we are in the presence of God in a way we have not experienced before. That torn Veil, reminding us of the broken and torn body of our Lord and Savior Jesus Christ, gives us access to this place where heaven meets earth, where the Creator communicates clearly with His creation. In the days of Moses, the priests donned a simple white linen robe to enter the Holy of Holies. We, too, lay aside ourselves when we come to Him here to worship and commune with Him. It is about who He is and not in any way about who we are.

SCRIPTURES

Psalm 24:3-5: *Who shall ascend into the hill of the Lord? or who shall stand in his Holy Place? He that hath clean hands, and a pure heart; who hath not lifted up his soul unto vanity, nor sworn deceitfully. He shall receive the blessing from the Lord, and righteousness from the God of his salvation.*

Psalm 15:1-5: *Lord, who shall abide in thy tabernacle? who shall dwell in thy holy hill? He that walketh uprightly, and worketh righteousness, and speaketh the truth in his heart. He that backbiteth not with his tongue, nor doeth evil to his neighbour, nor taketh up a reproach against his neighbour. In whose eyes a vile person is contemned; but he honoureth them that fear the Lord. He that sweareth to his own hurt, and changeth not. He that putteth not out his money to usury, nor taketh reward against the innocent. He that doeth these things shall never be moved.*

Matthew 27:51: *And, behold, the veil of the temple was rent in twain from the top to the bottom; and the earth did quake, and the rocks rent...*

Hebrews 4:16: *Let us therefore come boldly unto the throne of grace, that we may obtain mercy, and find grace to help in time of need.*

SONGS
"Holy Ground"(Geron Davis with The Pentecostals of Alexandria)
"In the Presence of Jehovah" (Geron and Becky Davis)
"Surely the Presence" (Lanny Wolfe)
"Shut in With God" (Traditional)
"Holy of Holies"(Tim Pedigo with The Pentecostals of Alexandria)

THINGS I PRAY IN THE HOLY OF HOLIES

Four Posts/The Gospels
> Pray the Beatitudes
> Pray the Parables
> Pray the Miracles

The Veil - the torn body of Jesus Christ gives us access to the Holy of Holies

Mercy Seat - His mercies are new every morning. Goodness and mercy follow us.

Manna – help us desire the Word and the strength that comes from the Word.

Ten Commandments – let me be an obedient servant.

Aaron's Rod – let me learn to move with the authority granted me by God's presence and anointing.

Let the Spirit pray for you and through you at this time.

MY PRAYER

This is a sensitive place. I take off my priestly garments and come before the throne of Almighty God. I am created one before my Creator; I am the redeemed sinner before my Savior. None of us is worthy to be in this place except for the blood and broken body of Jesus Christ, which purchased our access.

Holy God, we have been promised your presence. I am at this Veil and I have donned a white linen robe to come into Your presence. Nothing is here but You and me. I have walked through the posts symbolizing the four Gospel writers. Luke, the physician, the one who never saw You nor heard You speak but was compelled to tell Your story. Mark was a common man chosen by You to give the world and the ages some of the greatest writings in Your Word. Matthew, the reformed and redeemed tax collector told the world of You. And John the beloved, a fisherman who became a fisher of men. When I look at the Gospels, I see Your birth, Your life, Your death, Your burial, Your resurrection, Your ascension, and the promise of Your soon return.

As I study the beatitudes and the miracles and the parables, I want to be like You. Let me live the beatitudes. Let me expect the

miraculous. Let me practice the wisdom of the parables.
I want to reach for the less fortunate. Guide my steps. Lead me to someone who needs You. Lead me to a Matthew 25 person. Lead me to a Nicodemus who needs to know "except a man be born of water and spirit he cannot see the Kingdom of God" (John 3:5).

The priests of old applied blood to the Mercy Seat. I ask You to apply Your blood to me today. Your blood forgives all my sin. You are blinded by Your blood. You no longer see my failures and my faults, You see me through Your blood and I am yours. Thank You for Your mercy. Thank You for the power of Your forgiveness.

I go inside the Ark, and I am with Your presence – Your manna, Your Word. I pray Your ten commandments:

1) I love you with my whole heart.
2) I will put no god before you.
3) I will not take your name in vain.
4) I will honor my parents.
5) I will keep the Sabbath.
6) I will not murder. I will not assassinate people with my words. A three-inch tongue can slay a six-foot man. Do not let me be guilty of murder.
7) Keep me from adultery – keep my mind pure. Empower me by Your Holy Spirit to avoid all lust – physical, power, etc. Build walls around me and protect me. Guard my eyes, and guard my heart.
8) Don't let me covet the things you have given others.
9) Don't let me lie by word or deed, in action or implication. Let truth be in me.
10) Don't let me steal anything in any way. Do not let me take what does not belong to me. Let me always give of my tithes; I don't want to rob you. Let me be generous with my offerings that I not be a thief. (Malachi 3:8)

Thank You for the authority of Your name. It is matchless and mighty. Let me pray with the authority of Your name and power for my family and my church.

I smite sickness and disease.

I ask You to drive away divisive spirits.

Remove the things that hinder a free flow of Your Spirit among us.

Through Your name, Your Word, and Your blood, give me the courage to take authority over all that would come against me.

My Prayer In The Holy of Holies

_____

_____

_____

_____

_____

_____

_____

_____

_____

_____

_____

_____

_____

_____

_____

A FINAL NOTE...

Go back through the notes. Review the research. There was only one entrance to the Tabernacle. There was no exit. The entrance into the Tabernacle of Moses was also the exit from it.

We entered the courtyard with praise and thanksgiving. We repented and offered ourselves as the sacrifice on the Brazen Altar. We cleansed ourselves with the water of His word at the Laver of Water. We stepped through the columns into the Holy Place and stood in the light of the Golden Candlestick. We prayed over the Table of Shewbread and then, at the Altar of Incense, offered the sacrifice of praise. We stepped beyond the Veil into the Holy of Holies. We made our petitions known in the holy shekinah presence of God.

So, when we have completed our prayer journey, we make our way from our place of prayer in His presence to our place in the world in which He has called us and equipped us to live. We go into our world with songs and words and prayers of thanksgiving and praise flowing from us to the God who is worthy of it all.

Appendix A

The Songs of The Tabernacle

The Entrance Gate:
Traditional. *Praise Him.* Composer Unknown. Public Domain.

Taff, Russ. *Praise the Lord.* On *We Will Stand.* Bannister, Brown and Mike Hudson. Word Music, LLC, 1978. CD.

Williams, Kara with The Pentecostals of Alexandria Choir. *Waymaker.* Egbu, Osinachi Kalu Okoro. SLIC Inspire, 2016 https://youtu.be/KeXcHAurv5A , 2018. YouTube.

Truth. *Majesty.* On *Keeper of My Heart.* Hayford, Jack. New Spring, 1981. Paragon, 1982. VINYL.

Mangun, Mickey. *Total Praise.* On *The Message.* Smallwood, Richard. Bridge Building Music, Inc, T. Autumn Music (Admin by Brentwood-Benson Music Publishing, Inc), 1996. Past 12 Company, 2007. CD.

The Brazen Altar
Tomlin, Chris. *Give Us Clean Hands.* Hall, Charlie. On *Worship Together-Be Glorified.* 2000 Sixsteps Music. Capitol CMG Publishing. Sparrow Records, 2001. CD.

Traditional. *I Surrender All.* Van Deventer, Judson W and Winfield S. Weeden. 1896.

Traditional. *Just As I Am.* Elliott, Charlotte. 1835.

Munizzi, Martha. *Fill Me.* On *Make It Loud.* Munizzi, Martha and Daniel Eric Groves. Music Groves. Central South, 2011.

Smith, Kim Walker and Jesus Culture. *I Need You More.* On *Here Is Love.* Cooley, Lindell. Centergy Music, 1996. Bethel Music, 2010. CD.

THE LAVER OF WATER
Mercy Me. *Word of God Speak.* On *Spoken For.* Kipley, Pete and Bart Millard. Simpleville Music, Wordspring Music, LLC Songs From The Indigo Room, 2002. Columbia Records, 2002. CD

Mangun, Mickey. *Water Grave.* On *The* Message. Chapman, Steve. Monk and Tid Music. Past 12 Company, 2007. CD.

Phillips, Randy. *I Want to Be Holy.* Ariose Music, World of Pentecost Publishing, 1998.

Stampley, Micah. *Take My Life (Holiness).* On *The Songbook of Micah.* Underwood, Scott. Mercy/Vineyard Publishing, 1995. EMI Gospel, 2005.

THE HOLY PLACE
The Imperials. *His Name is Wonderful.* On *New Dimensions.* Mieir, Audrey. Manna Music, 1987. IMPACT, 1967. VINYL.

Yohe, Vicki. *Because of Who You Are.* On *I Just Want You.* Munizzi, Martha. Martha Munizzi Music, 2000. EMI Gospel/Pure Springs, 2003. CD.

Cory, Trent. *Mighty God.* On *Freedom Is.* Burt, James, Aaron Lindsey and Trent Cory. Warner-Tamerlane Publishing Corporation, 2008. Prayzhouse Records, 2008. CD.

Tomlin, Chris. *Good, Good Father.* On *Never Lose Sight.* Barrett, Pat and Anthony Brown. Pat Barrett music, Admin by Joseph Barrett, 2014. SixStep Records, 2016. CD.

Dubois, Cynthia McKellar with The Pentecostals of Alexandria Choir. *Peace Speaker.* Davis, Geron and Becky Davis. Meadowgreen Music Company, 1986. https://youtu.be/RvW3hStElV0 , 2013.

THE GOLDEN CANDLESTICK
Crabb, Jason. *Daystar.* On *Jason Crabb.* Richardson, Steve. Ariose Music, 1988. Springhill Music Group, 2009. CD.

Condon, Mark. *Welcome, Holy Spirit.*

Anderson, Jared. *Carrier.* On Live From My Church. Integrity Worship Music, 2009. Integrity Music, 2009.

Hillsong United. *Oceans (Where Feet May Fail).* On *Zion.* Croker, Matt, Joel Houston and Salomon Ligthelm. Hillsong Music Publishing, 2012. Hillsong, 2013.

Traditional. *Spirit of the Living God.* Iverson, Daniel. Birdwing Music, 1963.

The Martins. *He Leadeth Me.* On *Live In His Presence.* Gilmore, Joseph Henry and William Batchelder Bradbury. Public Domain. Spring Hill Group, 1995. CD.

THE TABLE OF SHEWBREAD
Rothwell, Randy. *Sanctuary (Lord Prepare Me).* On *Songs 4 Worship: Give You My Heart.* Scruggs, Randy and John W. Thompson. Full Armor Publishing Company, Whole Armor Publishing, 1982. Integrity Music, 2015. CD

Smith, Michael W. *Breathe*. On *Worship*. Barnett, Marie. Mercy/Vineyard Publishing, 1995. Reunion Records, 2011. CD.

Tomlin, Chris. *God of This City*. On *Hello Love*. Boyd, Aaron, Richard Bleakley, Peter Comfort, Ian Jordan, Peter Kernoghan and Andrew McCann. SixSteps Music, Admin. by Capitol CMG Publishing, 2006. SixSteps/Sparrow Records, 2008. CD

Mercy Me. *Word of God Speak*. On *Spoken For*. Kipley, Pete and Bart Millard. Simpleville Music, Wordspring Music, LLC Songs From The Indigo Room, 2002. Columbia Records, 2002. CD

THE ALTAR OF INCENSE
Anderson, Jared. *Hear Us From Heaven*. On *Where to Begin*. Integrity Worship Music, 2004. Integrity Media, 2006. CD.

Putnam, BJ. *Ask*. On *More and More Live*. Houghton, Israel, BJ Putnam and Jonathan Stockstill. Integrity's Praise! Music; Sound of The New Breed; Muskellunge Lake Muisc; DLD Music, 2012. Entertainment One Music, 2013. CD.

Baloche, Paul. *Offering (I Bring an Offering of Worship to My King)*. On *Offering of Worship*. Integrity's Hosanna! Music, 2002. Integrity Music, 2003. CD.

Moen, Don. *I Worship You Almighty God*. On *Worship With Don Moen*. Integrity's Hosanna! Music, Admin Capitol CMG Publishing, 1983. Integrity Music, 1992. CD.

Hillsong. *Like Incense (Sometimes By Step)*. On *A Beautiful Exchange*. Mullins, Richard and David Strasser. Hillsong, 2010. CD.

THE HOLY OF HOLIES

Davis, Geron with the Pentecostals of Alexandria Choir. *Holy Ground.* On *Holy Ground.* Songchannel Music, 1985. Integrity Music, 1994. CD.

Davis, Geron with POA the Pentecostals of Alexandria Choir. *In the Presence of Jehovah.* On *Holy Ground.* Davis, Becky and Geron Davis. Meadowgreen Music Company, 1985. Integrity Music, 1994. CD.

Wolfe, Lanny. *Surely the Presence of the Lord.* Lanny Wolfe Music, 1977.

Traditional. *Shut in With God.* Lillenas, Haldor. Nazarene Publishing House, 1948.

Tim Pedigo with the Pentecostals of Alexandria Choir. *Holy of Holies.* On *Holy Ground.* Davis, Geron Songchannel Music Company, 1985. Integrity Music, 1994 CD.

Made in the USA
Columbia, SC
25 April 2025